The New Americans
Recent Immigration and American Society

Edited by
Steven J. Gold and Rubén G. Rumbaut

A Series from LFB Scholarly

Undocumented and Unwanted
Attending College Against the Odds

Lisa D. Garcia

LFB Scholarly Publishing LLC
El Paso 2013

Copyright © 2013 by LFB Scholarly Publishing LLC

All rights reserved.

Library of Congress Cataloging-in-Publication Data

Garcia, Lisa DeAnn
    Undocumented and unwanted : attending college against the odds /
Lisa D. Garcia.
    pages cm -- (The new Americans: recent Immigration and
American society)
    Includes bibliographical references and index.
    ISBN 978-1-59332-701-9 (hardcover : alk. paper)
    1. Illegal aliens--Education (Higher)--United States. 2. Universities
and colleges--Residence requirements--United States. 3. Student aid--
United States. 4. College costs--United States. I. Title.
    LC3727.G37 2013
    378.1'982--dc23
                                              2013014954

ISBN 978-1-59332-701-9

Printed on acid-free 250-year-life paper.

Manufactured in the United States of America.

Table of Contents

List of Tables

Preface

Undocumented immigrant postsecondary students face myriad challenges while pursuing a college education. These overwhelmingly first-generation, low-income students lose their guarantee to a public education ensured by the 1982 *Plyler v. Doe* decision when they complete secondary school. They are foreclosed from traditional financial resources including federal, state, and institutional financial aid, scholarships, and employment opportunities. Students also are often under-prepared for the rigors of college-level coursework and may question the feasibility of pursuing a postsecondary degree with no legal protections. For those students who do manage to matriculate, few studies have been conducted to describe and better understand their experiences.

Framed by social capital theory, this qualitative study focused on the experiences of nine students attending a public comprehensive postsecondary institution in California. The study relied on data collected via interviews, observations, and document analysis throughout the 2009–2010 academic year to assess how different types of social capital helped students pursue a college education. This study demonstrated how students were wholly or partly reliant on various types of social capital accessed before and during matriculation. Three of the major findings included: (a) institutional agents were instrumental in developing students' social capital, (b) family- and peer-based social capital was important to students' matriculation, and (c) perceptions about immigration status affected students' matriculation and social capital development.

Acknowledgements

Many people have supported me throughout this project. First, I want to acknowledge the 40 students who participated in this study. Thank you for your time and your support. I appreciate your honesty and admire your hard work. I look forward to your continued success as responsible, caring, and productive adults.

I wish to thank William G. Tierney, Darnell Cole, and George J. Sanchez for their continued scholarly advice over the years. I extend many thanks to Leo Balk of LFB Scholarly as well as Steven J. Gold and Ruben G. Rumbaut, the series editors, for this opportunity. I want to thank Christina Garcia, George Garcia, Sara Garcia, Isaiah Garcia, Linda Bahrami, and members of the Consiglio, Galbero, and Reynaga families for their lifelong support.

Lastly, I want to thank my partner, Valentin Stoilov. That Warsaw Pact song I learned was an omen. You are a godsend. Merci.

CHAPTER ONE
An Introduction: Undocumented Immigrant College Students

The Monday before Veteran's Day 2009, 17 students assembled in a Metropolitan University (Metro U.)[1] classroom for a workshop on reinventing the undocumented immigrant story. Abel, former president of IMAGINE, the campus's undocumented student group, was leading the workshop. While he set up his laptop and projector, students excitedly talked about the upcoming school holiday. Jackie, the current IMAGINE president, explained, "With the furloughs, I haven't had a week where all of my classes meet. Next week they all meet ... so the extra day off is good for me." Across from Jackie, a recent transfer student confided in a friend sitting next to her. "I am not at that place where I am comfortable sharing my story. I hope we don't have to share our stories today." Jackie changed subjects to the undocumented immigrant symposium the group was co-hosting with a local non-profit organization later that week. "It'll be good. A local congresswoman may talk at the event. We won't know until the day before." A couple of students in the corner checked their e-mail and Facebook accounts.

Abel called the meeting to order. Not all of the attendees were ready to start the meeting. "I think we should wait another 10 minutes," exclaimed Luz, the current IMAGINE vice president. "Yeah, you moved the meeting, so we should wait for students to get over here,"

---

[1] All of the names and other identifiable information that appear in this book are pseudonyms.

1

suggested another student. Five minutes later, Abel called the group to attention and started his presentation. Several students quietly wrapped up the food they were eating and the room settled down.

Abel worked with a statewide community-based political organization focused on developing a greater voice for working-class and immigrant communities in California. He made this presentation to community-based groups interested in re-conceptualizing the national immigration debate. IMAGINE invited him to speak so as to give its membership some new ideas about how to talk about students' individual immigration situations. Abel posed a question to the room, "Anyone have any ideas why we haven't had immigration reform since 1986?" One girl muttered under her breath, "They hate us." Another student offered, "It's not a priority." One of the students working on his laptop exclaimed, "They'd rather build a wall then deal with it." Abel smiled and offered another reason. "We use the same tactics that they used in the 1960s to demand their rights. I don't relate to it. You don't relate to it …. We have to relate to citizens. We can do that with our stories."

There were puzzled looks from half of the students while the other students nodded in agreement. Abel continued, "What do you say to a person who calls you [as an undocumented immigrant] a lawbreaking, uneducated, lazy, welfare recipient who doesn't speak English?" Luz sarcastically interrupted, "You forgot the word 'alien' cause you know we're all like E.T." The students laughed. Abel changed his tone. "You say to these people that we are loyal, hardworking, family-oriented, honest, and hopeful people who are pursuing our dreams. We want to be part of this country. We want to make America great and strong."

The audience was silent for a few moments. A recent transfer student raised his hand to speak. "It's different but I think this can work. I am not undocumented but I can use this type of thing when I tell people about you guys. It's positive, not whiny." Another student posed the question, "Do you really think someone like Lou Dobbs would listen to that story?" Luz's hand quickly shot up. "But how do we do this if we have been trained by other organizations to demand our rights? You know, go picket, and yell and tell people you demand to be made legal." Attendees quickly started to agree with Luz. Abel motioned for the group to come back together. "That's what we are going to talk about today—how do we tell America that we are students and not aliens. We're talking about how we tell our stories."

Undocumented immigrants enroll in postsecondary institutions around the country. Like Metro U., a handful of these institutions have a sizeable undocumented immigrant population. On these campuses, undocumented students gather to form student support groups and raise awareness about undocumented issues that directly affect their ability to pursue a postsecondary education. With or without these groups, many undocumented students take on advocacy roles in their communities and on their campuses. Students access and enact social capital within their peer groups, on campus, and in their larger communities in order to fulfill their postsecondary goals. In the remainder of this chapter, I outline this study's purpose and significance as well as the research questions I address. I then provide an overview of undocumented students pursuing a college education before presenting the theoretical framework that guides this study. Finally, I give a brief description of the study location and participants.

PURPOSE AND SIGNIFICANCE OF THE STUDY
Purpose
Undocumented immigrants are a legally-banned category of immigrants as they lack the required documentation to reside lawfully in the United States (De Genova, 2002, 2004). Passel and Cohn (2009) define undocumented immigrants as "[consisting] of residents of the United States who are not U.S. citizens, who do not hold current permanent resident visas, or who have not been granted permission under a set of specific authorized temporary statuses for longer-term residence and work" (p. vi). Most undocumented immigrants enter the US without valid documents or arrive with valid visas but remain in the US after their visas expire and/or violate the terms of their visas. Some undocumented immigrants later obtain temporary authorization to live and work in the country (Passel & Cohn, 2011). As many as 10% of undocumented immigrants hold temporary protected status (TPS) or have filed for asylum status. Many of these quasi-legal individuals could revert to undocumented status at any point. As of March 2011, there are approximately 11.1 million undocumented immigrants residing in the US (Passel & Cohn, 2012; Pew Hispanic Center, 2013). Of this total, approximately one million are children (Passel & Cohn, 2011; Pew Hispanic Center, 2013).

While the academic literature focusing on documented immigrant postsecondary students' experiences in college is limited (Bailey &

Weininger, 2002; Conway, 2009; Zhou, 1997), research on the unique situation of undocumented students is even sparser (Abrego, 2008; Perez, 2009, 2012; Perez & Cortez, 2011; Perez, Espinoza, Ramos, Coronado, & Cortes, 2009). Current research on undocumented students primarily focuses on basic demographic information and statistics (e.g., Batalova & Fix, 2006; Gonzales, 2007, 2009; Passel, 2003, 2005; Passel & Cohn, 2008, 2009). Researchers are still orienting themselves with the population by chronicling where students attend and how they finance college. Other recent scholarly work employs quantitative methods to measure college students' resilience and persistence (Flores, 2010; Flores & Horn, 2009; Perez et al., 2009).

Scholars know that completing a college education is a challenge for undocumented students since they lack the legal residency or citizenship required for federal and state financial aid and most scholarships (Abrego, 2008; Perez, 2009, 2012; Perez & Cortez, 2011; Perez et al., 2009; Rincon, 2008). Previous research also details how undocumented students living underground develop political, legal, and social consciousness that fosters college attendance and political activism (Abrego, 2006, 2008; Negron-Gonzalez, 2009; Orner, 2008; Perez, 2012; Perez, Espinoza, Ramos, Coronado, & Cortes, 2010; Seif, 2004). Researchers know less about how exactly students pursue postsecondary degrees at four-year institutions. They do not know how students overcome academic, financial, and personal issues in pursuing their academic goals.

Thus, the purpose of this study is to understand how undocumented students create personal and communal identities that foster the development of social capital that in turn helps them attend four-year institutions. I explore how students overcome personal and societal challenges to their sense of belonging and inclusion in American society. The study also examines how students are similar and different to their low-income and first-generation college student peers. The reality of being undocumented while attending K–12 schools and preparing for four-year university admission influences how a student perceives one's future academic and career goals. Undocumented immigration status shapes the types of support and encouragement—personal, state, and federal—students receive in pursuing postsecondary goals. The study expands the current understanding about how these students: (a) conceptualize themselves within the undocumented immigration debate, (b) identify themselves among other low-income and first-generation students, (c) and shape their educational goals working within a current system that does not guarantee or fully support their access to a postsecondary education.

Significance
Researchers have only recently begun to generate detailed data for school age undocumented immigrants (Passel & Cohn, 2009). Passel (2003) estimates that approximately 65,000 undocumented immigrants who have lived in the US for five or more years graduate from high school each year. The children of undocumented immigrants—both those who are undocumented and those who are U.S. citizens—make up 6.8% of the students enrolled in the nation's K–12 schools. About one-third of these children live in poverty, nearly double the rate for children of U.S.-born parents. Further, approximately 40% of the undocumented ages 18 to 24 have not completed secondary school, compared to 15% of legal immigrants and 8% of U.S.-born residents. This data supports the adult undocumented data—undocumented students are more prone to poverty and lower levels of education.

Most undocumented immigrants are optimistic about attaining a higher level of education in the US than in their homelands (Suarez-Orozco & Suarez-Orozco, 2001). Within this under-educated and impoverished group, there are students who pursue a college education. Of the undocumented ages 18 to 24 who completed high school, 49% are in college or have attended college; those who arrived in the US at ages 14 or older have a 42% college-going rate whereas those who arrived before age 14 have a 61% rate. According to the National Immigration Law Center (2009), the college-going rate is between 5% and 10% for all undocumented students who graduate from high school. In California, the state with the largest undocumented population, policymakers and politicians estimate that as many as 20,000 students enroll on a part- or full-time basis in the state's public postsecondary institutions each year (Batalova & Fix, 2006; Passel, 2005; Passel & Cohn, 2009, 2011). Recent estimates of undocumented beneficiaries of California Assembly Bill 540 (AB 540)[2] total

---

[2] California Assembly Bill 540 (AB 540) grants some undocumented students in-state academic fees based on long-term residency and high school completion.

approximately 1% or less of all students enrolled in California's three public postsecondary systems (Ferriss, 2010). As of this printing, 13 states and/or postsecondary systems (California, Connecticut, Illinois, Kansas, Maryland, Nebraska, New Mexico, New York, Oklahoma, Rhode Island, Texas, Washington, and Utah) have established undocumented-friendly tuition policies. Batalova and Fix (2006) state that there may be as many as 50,000 college students nationwide. All of these figures are estimates since most institutions do not require immigration documentation for enrollment purposes (Abrego, 2008; Hermes, 2008).

The *Plyler v. Doe* (1982) decision ensures that undocumented children receive a K–12 education but stops short of declaring public education a fundamental right (Olivas, 2005, 2012; Seif, 2004). School districts nationwide enroll K–12 students without questioning immigration status; hence, the majority of undocumented students receive a primary and secondary education (Olivas, 2009, 2012). They enroll in the same courses, engage in the same activities, and compete for the same awards, distinctions, and grades as their documented and U.S.-born peers (Madera et al., 2008; Orner, 2008). Like their peers, some undocumented students aspire to continue their education past high school and prepare for college admission (Gonzales, 2007, 2009; Madera et al., 2008). However, there is no federal legislation or court ruling that ensures these same students receive a postsecondary education.

This book provides a more detailed account of what undocumented students face when they reach a four-year institution. Focusing on one campus with a significant undocumented population, I describe the reality of undocumented postsecondary students in one geographic area. Examining undocumented students' college preparation and matriculation may better inform the academic literature devoted to increasing college access and completion for the one million undocumented children residing in the US (Passel & Cohn, 2011; Pew Hispanic Center, 2013).

RESEARCH QUESTIONS

To understand the intersection between undocumented students' experiences of exclusion and illegality and their pursuit of an unguaranteed higher education within the context of a social capital theoretical framework, I am guided by four research questions:

1. How do undocumented college students develop, maintain, and exchange social capital?
2. Do the social support networks of undocumented college students factor into educational outcomes?
3. How do experiences of exclusion shape the educational identity and consciousness of undocumented students?
4. How do the contours of an undocumented student's identity enable or disable academic performance?

SOCIAL CAPITAL THEORY

As I elaborate in Chapter 2, undocumented students encounter numerous obstacles en route to earning a postsecondary degree. Their immigration status poses particular financial, academic, and personal problems that for the majority of undocumented students are insurmountable. When coupled with the reality that they have little if no formal support from the national, state, and institutional levels to cope with these issues, undocumented college students' postsecondary trajectories are complicated matters. Most students do not attend college without significant and continued support of peers, relatives, and institutional agents. These individuals and groups provide students with the necessary social capital in which to complete a college degree.

Social capital theory is a multidisciplinary concept useful in explaining why particular individuals are more successful in accessing educational resources and achieving academic goals. The theory helps account for how social relationships and the resources connected to students directly affect them as they navigate educational and social institutions. Social capital refers to the connections and resources within and between social networks that allow individuals and groups to achieve goals. Investment in social networks as well as in mutual recognition and acknowledgment fosters goal achievement. The underlying assumption in social capital theory is that networks and group affiliations are likely to positively influence the acquisition of relevant social capital resources.

For this study, I focus on two distinct versions of social capital theory—bridging and bonding. The "bridging" variety proposed by sociologist Pierre Bourdieu (1986) stresses the importance of individuals accessing social capital normally held outside of the close relationships and networks found within families and peer groups. This heterogeneous type of social capital fosters a broader network of group affiliations by which an individual can access resources. The "bonding" variety of social capital proposed by another sociologist, James Coleman (1988, 1990), focuses on the importance of individuals accessing social capital held inside of the close relationships formed in familial and kin groups. This homogenous type of social capital develops norms and social control that individual members follow yet does not facilitate accessing resources held outside of the group. Both Bourdieu's and Coleman's versions of social capital theory are useful in examining how undocumented immigrants successfully attend four-year postsecondary institutions.

This theoretical approach allows for an understanding of individual undocumented students' circumstances, experiences, and actions when pursuing a college education. Social capital theory helps delineate which types of social capital—bridging or bonding—help students at different periods during their academic trajectories. Further, the theory highlights how factors such as weak and strong social ties with different actors provide students with diverse and malleable resources that ultimately help them reach their academic goals. Understanding how students procure and activate such resources is important in understanding how they attend college.

SITE SELECTION AND RESEARCH PARTICIPANTS
Chapter 3 discusses the site selection and research participants in detail. Here, I provide a brief summary of the primary site and the research participants. This serves as an introduction, but more importantly provides context for the discussion of undocumented students in the following chapters.

The University of California (UC) and the California State University (CSU) are California's two four-year public universities. Under the California Master Plan, the UC selects from among the top one-eighth (12.5%) and the CSU selects from the top one-third (33.3%) of the state's high school graduating class (University of California, 2007). The UC is the state's primary research university, conferring bachelor's, master's, and doctoral degrees across disciplines. The CSU primarily focuses on undergraduate education, granting both bachelor's and master's degrees in technical and academic subjects.

I collected data from a total of 40 UC and CSU undocumented students. While data collected from all of the 40 study participants informed the results of the study, this study primarily focuses on the lives of nine undocumented students attending Metropolitan University (Metro U.), a single CSU campus. Their stories are presented later in Chapter 4. Metro U. is located in a metropolitan area in California. The university enrolls over 15,000 undergraduates and 5,000 graduate students; approximately 25% and 55% of student enrollees attend part-time respectively. The majority—approximately 85% of Metro U. matriculants—are California residents. Qualified Metro U. students—both documented and undocumented—may take advantage of reduced in-state academic fees via AB 540 legislation. The annual 2009–2010 in-state academic fees for Metro U. were $4,893.

Metro U. enrolls undocumented students as evidenced by the campus's undocumented student support group as well as published undocumented enrollee estimates (Ferriss, 2010). Also, the metropolitan area where Metro U. is located is home to the largest undocumented immigrant population in the nation—approximately one million residents (Hill & Hayes, 2013; Pastor & Ortiz, 2009). Considering that Metro U. is less academically competitive and costs less money to attend than other area four-year postsecondary institutions, the actual Metro U. population of undocumented students is assumed to be larger than the sample of Metro U. students interviewed for this study.

Study participants included self-identified UC, CSU, and Metro U. undocumented immigrant students. I located and identified 40 student participants—12 UC, three CSU, and 25 Metro U. students—using "snowball sampling" (Salganik & Heckathorn, 2004; Watters & Biernacki, 1989). The study included students who started their postsecondary academic careers as freshmen or transfer students. Students were not chosen based on area of study, gender, or racial/ethnic/national background. Rather, students were chosen based on their interest in the study and ability to participate. Study participants received no compensation for their participation.

ORGANIZATION OF THE BOOK
In the following chapter, I provide a more detailed examination of the literature on undocumented college students and social capital theory. In Chapter 3, I discuss the methodological framework of this study. Chapter 4 contains an exploration of undocumented students' experiences as they relate to social capital theory discussed in Chapter 2. In the final chapter, I offer discussion and analysis of the data and

consider the ways in which a focus on social capital informs the literature on undocumented students.

CHAPTER TWO

Conceptual Framework

Dusk was fast approaching on an unusually balmy evening in late November. Alejandra and I sat on the arts patio discussing her experiences in college. She explained in detail how she paid for her postsecondary education without access to state and federal financial aid programs.

> I pay for college with scholarships and my own earnings. Actually, the first three years I've had scholarships …. People have helped me, too. My best friend was coming here in the beginning and now he is in the Navy. He was very supportive of my situation. I will never forget what he did. Every time he would get extra financial aid, he would give it to me. I would get like $300 or he would pay for my school books. I was just like … I never expected a friend my own age paying for my books. He was like, "I understand your situation and I want to help you out."

Alejandra elaborated that this friend likely enrolled at Metropolitan University (Metro U.) because she enrolled. "He wasn't that much into school. I think he wanted to help me out more than go to college." She also paid for school with the help of a family friend.

> My sponsor, you know this family friend of ours… so his proposal … we wrote a contract, too …. My senior year, I have two options. He will either pay for my full senior

academic year—tuition, books, graduation. If I have a scholarship to cover that, he will get me a student apartment and cover my living expenses.

Alejandra was already working on scholarship applications for the next fall term since she wanted to take advantage of his offer to pay for her living expenses. She explained that if he pays for her living expenses the following year, "it will help [her] focus on [her] studies and not be distracted [like she is] at home."

As Alejandra and I continued to talk, she told me that she is confident that her undocumented status has not prevented her from pursuing her educational and career goals. Though, she did recognize that if she was not resourceful and persistent in pursuing her goals, she likely would not be enrolled at Metro U. She reflected on her journey leading up to her attendance at Metro U. In high school, she transferred to a new public high school at the beginning of her junior year in search of educational opportunities that would better prepare her for a postsecondary education. She graduated as valedictorian of her class and had been involved in school, community, and political awareness campaigns and projects since middle school. During her secondary and postsecondary careers, she has relied on the teachings of Paulo Freire and Karl Marx for inspiration and direction in pursuing her goals.

As I elaborate in Chapter 4, Alejandra is typical of many students at Metro U.—she is Latina, grew up in the surrounding community, and was identified as college-bound early in her academic career. Alejandra is also the first in her immediate family to attend college and comes from a low socioeconomic background. She has consistently earned top grades in college and has made steady progress towards her degree in social work. She wants to earn an advanced degree and pursue a career as a social worker. Although most of her college peers would never assume that Alejandra is an undocumented immigrant, her immigration status has affected much of her college career. In response to the obstacles and limitations that Alejandra has encountered due to her immigration status, she has procured and activated sources of social capital in order to find alternative means to attend college.

This study focuses on how undocumented immigrants actively pursue a postsecondary education at a four-year institution. I have designed a study that analyzes the ways undocumented students successfully pursue their academic goals without any legal guarantees or formal support from the federal and state governments. I seek to understand how students gather the resources necessary to complete their degrees.

In this chapter, I discuss the challenges that undocumented immigrants face as they pursue a postsecondary degree. I also include specific contextual information as it applies to Metro U. students. In response to these challenges, I apply social capital theory in addressing the study's four primary research questions. I review the basic tenets of social capital theory and the views of the theory's primary architects. Next, I discuss how the strength of social ties as well as how internal and external factors shape students' acquisition of social capital. I then present the shortcomings of this theoretical approach and place the theory within the context of a study of undocumented postsecondary students. Finally, I elaborate on the study's primary research questions and how applying social capital theory helps answer the questions.

UNDOCUMENTED STUDENTS' COLLEGE-GOING CHALLENGES

While most undocumented immigrants are optimistic about attaining a higher level of education in the US than in their homelands (Suarez-Orozco & Suarez-Orozco, 2001), many find it difficult to finish a postsecondary degree. Given that they are not guaranteed access to a college education, the route to college is conditional and uncertain for many of these students (Abrego, 2006, 2008; Gonzales, 2007, 2009; Perez, 2012). Academic literature focusing on documented immigrant students' experiences in college is limited (Bailey & Weininger, 2002; Conway, 2009; Zhou, 1997); research on the unique situation of undocumented students is even sparser (Abrego, 2008; Perez et al., 2009). Research documenting the challenges low-income and first-generation college students encounter along with the available undocumented literature provides some insight about how these students engage in the college-going process. Scholars present three main challenges undocumented college students experience in pursuing a college education: financial obstacles, academic preparation, and perceptions of belonging.

Financial Obstacles

Education scholars cite financial obstacles as a primary reason why undocumented immigrants find it challenging, if not impossible, to pursue a postsecondary education (Abrego, 2006, 2008; Flores, 2010; Garcia & Tierney, 2011; Gonzales, 2007, 2009; Oliverez, 2006; Perez, 2009, 2012). The majority of undocumented students hail from low-income, working-class families that are not in the position to solely finance a college education. Low-income students are particularly conscious of the human, economic, and social costs involved in the decision to go to college (Perna, 2005). They consider the total cost of a college education including foregone earnings and leisure time as well as direct college expenses. As a result, low-income students are less likely to apply to college (Gladieux & Swail, 1999).

Undocumented students find themselves in the same general predicament as other low-income students. Conscious of the human and financial costs of attending college, they often forego college enrollment so that they can better help support their families. Since the majority of their older relatives are constrained to low-paying jobs in the service sector where immigration status is not scrutinized (Chavez, 1998), students generally choose to work on a full-time basis so that they can contribute to household expenses. Students also frequently take on more significant responsibilities in caring for younger siblings and managing daily household duties as older relatives may be forced to work longer hours at non-traditional times. For many undocumented students and their families, pursuing a postsecondary education is considered a luxury that is neither necessary nor economically viable. This said, there are a handful of undocumented immigrants that do transition to college. Those who do matriculate confront three primary financial obstacles—exclusion from traditional financial aid programs, limited employment opportunities, and restricted alternative funding sources.

Undocumented students are ineligible for state and federal financial aid and most scholarships since legal residency or citizenship is a prerequisite for qualification (Perez, 2012; Perez et al., 2009). Unlike their citizen and documented immigrant peers, undocumented immigrants cannot rely on federal and state grant, scholarship, loan, and work study programs to partially or fully pay their academic costs. Instead, they and their families must pay out of pocket the full costs of their postsecondary education. Researchers argue that higher levels of financial aid generally correlate with higher college enrollment rates for low-income students (Heller, 1997, 1999; Kane, 1999; St. John, 2003, 2006). Without access to financial aid, many undocumented immigrants do not consider a higher education a realistic goal and instead pursue low-paying jobs where immigration status is not closely monitored (Hermes, 2008). Financing a postsecondary education without traditional financial aid resources is a significant undertaking for undocumented college students (Gonzales, 2007, 2009).

In response to undocumented students being foreclosed from traditional state and federal financial aid programs, pro-immigrant activists have advocated for two primary forms of financial assistance for students—reduced in-state academic fees and legislation allowing undocumented immigrants access to financial aid and a path to citizenship. Thirteen states and postsecondary systems have successfully passed legislation and policies that offer reduced in-state academic fees at public postsecondary institutions to certain undocumented immigrants. These lower-fee policies meet the criteria outlined in the 1996 Illegal Immigration Reform and Immigrant Responsibility Act (IIRIRA). IIRIRA maintains that states cannot offer higher education benefits to undocumented students without offering the same benefits to U.S. citizens and legal residents. IIRIRA does not constitute a federal ban on undocumented students attending college, but does restrict what individual states can do to make higher education more accessible to undocumented students.

California offers certain undocumented immigrant students access to lower in-state academic fees via California Assembly Bill 540 (AB 540). AB 540 went into effect in January 2002 and provides in-state fees to select citizens, legal residents, and undocumented immigrants based on their length of state residence, graduation from an in-state high school, and age at time of immigration. As presented in Chapter 4, the majority of undocumented Metro U. students pay in-state fees. AB 540 has had a significant impact on undocumented immigrants enrolled at California public postsecondary institutions (Abrego, 2008; Perez, 2012). However, even with access to in-state fees, a higher education is still an overwhelming monetary expense for most undocumented students and their families (Gonzales, 2009).

The second form of assistance pro-immigrant activists have advocated for is both federal and state legislation allowing undocumented immigrants access to federal and state financial aid. The federal Development, Relief, and Education for Alien Minors (DREAM) Act is proposed federal legislation that would provide some undocumented immigrants a path to permanent residency and open access to federal financial aid given they fulfill certain education or military commitments. The United States Congress has considered various forms of the legislation since 2001. The federal DREAM Act most recently failed to gain the support of both chambers of Congress in December 2010.

Several states have also attempted to pass similar state legislation that would allow undocumented students access to various state and institutional financial aid programs. In 2011, California Governor Jerry Brown signed California Assembly Bill 130 and 131. This legislation, commonly referred to as the California DREAM (Development, Relief, and Education for Alien Minors) Act, allows those undocumented students who qualify for reduced in-state fees via California AB 540 to access institutional (AB 130) and state (AB 131) financial aid. Implementation of AB 130 and AB 131 began in 2011 and 2013 respectively. The students chronicled in this book did not have access to the institutional and state financial aid provided by the California Dream Act (AB 130 and AB 131) and thus were foreclosed from a significant amount of financial aid.

Another financial obstacle undocumented students experience concerns employment restrictions. Most undocumented college students do not have legal permission to work in the US. Even if students do secure employment to help finance their education before and/or during college, jobs are usually off campus, low paying, and concentrated in the service industry (Hermes, 2008; Perez et al., 2009; Suarez-Orozco & Suarez-Orozco, 2001). These jobs often require long commutes and inconsistent, non-traditional working hours that make attending college difficult (Garcia & Tierney, 2011). Students' limited employment opportunities affect how much money they can apply to their education-related expenses. Saving enough money to pay full academic fees at four-year institutions as well as paying for books, transportation, and living expenses is an overwhelming task for many college-bound undocumented students.

In 2012, President Barack Obama announced a new program—Deferred Action for Childhood Arrivals (DACA)—that would provide relief from deportation for eligible undocumented immigrants who are ages 30 and under and arrived in the US before age 16. DACA recipients would also receive permission to legally work in the US. Demographers estimate that nearly 1.7 million qualified undocumented immigrants could benefit from the program (Passel & Lopez, 2012).

Some of the students in this study have since qualified for DACA and have received permission to work legally in the US. This program was not available when the data was gathered for this study.

The third financial obstacle concerns undocumented students' access to alternative funding sources such as undocumented-friendly scholarships, stipends, and sponsors. Many of these funding sources require students to provide proof of citizenship or legal residency for eligibility. Since many undocumented students discover their legal status during the college application process, they are unable to find alternative funding sources that provide money to undocumented immigrants before transitioning to college (National Immigration Law Center, 2009). Even those students who are aware of their status are disadvantaged since alternative funding sources are limited and usually highly competitive (Madera et al., 2008). Few students can rely on these funding sources to pay for all of their college-related expenses.

Funding a college education is burdensome for the majority of undocumented immigrants. Even a student who is able to pay reduced in-state academic fees, save money, and secure scholarships finds it challenging to pursue a college education. As a result, most undocumented students originally bound for four-year institutions usually opt for enrollment at two-year institutions because of reduced costs (Hermes, 2008). Enrolling at a two-year college creates another hurdle since some education scholars believe that beginning a postsecondary education at a two-year institution decreases a student's chances of obtaining a bachelor's degree (Dougherty, 1987; Grubb, 1991; Shaw, 1997). As a result, only a fraction of academically-eligible students can financially afford to attend college (Gonzales, 2009). Even fewer successfully graduate with a degree from a four-year institution.

Academic Preparation
The academic preparation of undocumented college students is another substantial obstacle in the journey towards a postsecondary degree. Competing with better-prepared and -informed students is challenging to undocumented students already burdened with paying out of pocket for college. Attending low-performing schools, being a first-generation student, and facing personal obstacles are three hurdles many undocumented students have to overcome in order to continue their education.

Undocumented students, like other low-income students, often attend low-performing, ethnically-isolated schools located in concentrated pockets of urban, inner-city communities (Gandara, 1995; Gonzales, 2009; Teranishi & Briscoe, 2006). Violence is more prevalent in the schools and neighborhoods, distracting students from their academic studies and limiting extracurricular activities due to safety concerns (Perez et al., 2009). These schools have less-qualified teachers, offer fewer college preparation courses, and receive less funding (Abrego, 2006).

Attending low-performing and less-rigorous schools has a negative impact on overall college readiness. Adelman (2006) points to the rigor of high school coursework as a leading indicator of college readiness at high school graduation. Students who lack strong English language skills are at a significant disadvantage in college compared to their well-prepared peers (Adelman, 1996, 1998). This disadvantage is especially relevant for immigrant students who are more likely to face a language barrier and enroll in English as a Second Language (ESL) courses in college (Casas-Frier & Hansen, 2006; Keller, 2001). Scholars also found that when students require significant remediation when they transition to college, they may be less inclined to spend the extra time preparing for college-level courses (Melguizo, Hagedorn, & Cypers, 2008). For undocumented students, this situation is compounded by the fact that they do not receive financial assistance to take these extra remedial courses.

Undocumented college students are also frequently the first in their families to attend college (Gonzales, 2009; Perez et al., 2009). First-generation college students rely on institutional actors more for comprehensive college information, since their families are less likely to provide college-preparation information at home (Stanton-Salazar, 1997). Moreover, inner-city and low-performing high schools generally have fewer college-going networks among the student body. Staff and faculty at these schools typically focus more on graduation rates, standardized testing, and truancy issues than college attendance (Teranishi & Briscoe, 2006; Tierney & Venegas, 2006). Focusing on these issues rather than college access contributes to low-income and first-generation students not receiving academic information about college in a timely manner. This situation is even more severe for undocumented students since they are unable to participate in some college preparation and mentoring programs due to their immigration status (Gonzales, 2009). First-generation undocumented college students thus are more prone to arrive at postsecondary institutions with less experience, knowledge, and resources about how to successfully matriculate.

Academic preparation during high school or even earlier is not always a linear trajectory for undocumented students. Some students experience a sense of despair during their educational careers and withdraw from school activities (Gonzalez, Plata, Garcia, Torres, & Urrieta, 2003; Suarez-Orozco & Suarez-Orozco, 2001); students no longer strive for academic and extracurricular distinctions, letting their grades fall and discontinuing their extracurricular activities. This despair usually occurs during high school when students begin to realize the limitations they will encounter in society as undocumented adults. Even as college students, they will encounter many of the same barriers that undocumented family members and friends encounter in securing employment. These lapses in motivation have deleterious effects on students' abilities to prepare for and attend college. The students who make it to college indicate that they are not as competitive and prepared for admission or funding opportunities due to their past withdrawal from academics (Suarez-Orozco & Suarez-Orozco, 2001). Preparing to transition to college as an undocumented immigrant can be challenging without the purposeful help and intervention of key institutional agents who can help remedy academic deficiencies.

Perceptions of Belonging
A third challenge undocumented college students suffer concerns their perceptions of belonging within U.S. society. Much of the legitimacy and sense of belonging in the US that undocumented students lose over time is directly related to their transition from K–12 schooling to college. The formal K–12 system that defines undocumented immigrants as students also facilitates their inclusion and indoctrination into U.S. society (Abrego, 2006; Lopez, 2003). Students learn the history, culture, and language of the US through their formal education. The transition to college and adulthood can dismantle perceptions of personal, institutional, and societal inclusion that are important to successful matriculation.

Feeling "included" as an undocumented student amid constant academic, personal, and financial obstacles is important to student success (Perez Huber, 2009). Individual feelings of inclusion are diminished as undocumented students transition from a childhood with a guaranteed K–12 education to an adulthood with no educational guarantees. The coping mechanisms they develop in order to feel normal and legitimate are essential to their success as college students (Perez et al., 2009). For example, periodic questioning of inclusion can begin when undocumented college students are not able to drive a car or attend a school-sponsored trip that requires long-distance or international travel. Students may also have to answer questions from peers about why they attend a community college instead of a four-year institution, why they cannot go to a nightclub that requires identification for entry, or why they took a term off from school to work on a full-time basis. Constant questions about perceived "abnormal" social or college-going behaviors hinder personal feelings of inclusion in a society that at times intentionally and unintentionally excludes undocumented students from age-appropriate social and academic activities (Perez et al., 2009; Perez Huber, 2009).

Scholars also highlight the importance of ethnic and racial minority students feeling included and welcomed in educational institutions as a prerequisite for student success (Allen & Solorzano, 2001; Blackwell, 1981; Contreras, 2009; Hurtado, Milem, Clayton-Pedersen & Allen, 1999; Solorzano, Allen, & Carroll, 2002). For undocumented students who are mostly ethnic and racial minorities, inclusion goes beyond diversity at the institutional level. Abrego (2008) explains that undocumented students' feelings of inclusion on college campuses are constantly under threat since their immigration status is equivalent to illegality. Contreras (2009) describes how some undocumented students have negative experiences with institutional staff members. For many students their illegality translates into a vulnerable, inferior status within the larger society and among their college peers (Abrego, 2008; Olivas, 2009); even if they have a record of academic excellence, they still may feel that they do not have the same rights as U.S.-born residents and documented immigrants to attend college. Believing that one deserves a higher education is important for undocumented students' success in achieving their postsecondary goals.

Finally, undocumented college students question whether they are a part of the larger society. Undocumented immigrants frequently live in the shadows of society due to the legal issues that accompany their immigration status (Chavez, 1998). Abrego (2008) explains that "their status is a constant reminder that they [are] different, vulnerable, and considered suspect" (p. 723) within their local and national communities. Even though they are long-standing members of the community, they are still considered outsiders by a national legal system that assigns different rights to citizens and aliens (Marshall, 1998). Their status as undocumented immigrants amounts to a life of official exclusion from the political and social environments they inhabit (Abrego, 2008; Olivas, 2009; Seif, 2004).

Perceptions of feeling unwelcome in society overwhelm many undocumented immigrants (Perez Huber, 2009; Perry, 2006). Feelings of difference and being an outsider accompany immigrants' fears of deportation, isolation, and depression (Contreras, 2009; Dozier, 1993; Hart, 1997; Perez, 2009, 2012; Perez et al., 2009; Perry, 2006). Isolation from the larger community limits contact with individuals and organizations in a position to assist undocumented students with accomplishing their goals. In the case of low-income and first-generation students, relationships with peers are pivotal since they lack other social relationships and resources that foster successful college matriculation (Dennis, Phinney, & Chuateco, 2005; Hurtado, Carter, & Spuler, 1996; Stanton-Salazar & Dornbusch, 1995). Many undocumented college students modify their academic and social activities in order to minimize the possibility of being identified as undocumented by school officials or law enforcement (Perez, 2009). Refraining from communal social activities limits the opportunities when these students can make friends and meet contacts who can possibly assist with educational plans. Feelings of inclusion in the community facilitate undocumented students bridging networks of people and resources that may assist with their educational goals.

Undocumented immigrants endure significant challenges while pursuing a college education. The economic, academic, and personal issues they must overcome before and during matriculation leaves many students unable to finish their degree programs. This study explores how undocumented students overcome such obstacles and successfully pursue their college goals. In particular, students procure sources of social capital during their secondary and postsecondary educations that enable them to attend and remain in college. What follows is a discussion of social capital theory. I discuss the basic tenets of the theory and provide insight about how students benefit from using social capital in pursuing their academic goals.

SOCIAL CAPITAL

The notion of capital is often constrained to economic discussions of surplus value and resources. Social scientists offer their own definitions of capital in concordance with their specific area of capital-related research. Sociologist Pierre Bourdieu (1986) defines capital as the

> accumulated labor (in its materialized form or its 'incorporated,' embodied form) which, when appropriated on a private, i.e., exclusive, basis by agents or groups of agents, enables them to appropriate social energy in the form of reified or living labor. (p. 241)

Capital takes time to accumulate and can be spent, exchanged, expanded, contracted, lost, or recaptured within groups and societies (Tierney, 2006).

Classic economic theories state that capital remains a surplus value and represents an investment with expected returns (Lin, 1999). Further, capital benefits an actor within a group as an individual cannot acquire or exchange capital with oneself. Karl Marx (1849/1978) believed that the examination of capital was mostly limited to the structural or class level and was intimately associated with the exploitation of classes within a capitalist system. As social scientists appropriated the classical definition of capital and expanded on its concepts to better fit their own work, three primary "neo-capital" theories emerged—human, cultural, and social (Lin, 1999).

Human capital theory conceives capital as an investment. Human capital is a means of production in which additional investment yields additional output (Becker, 1993). For instance, an individual can invest in human capital via education or specialized training in hopes of negotiating with those in control of the production process (an employer) for an economic payment. Human capital is similar to the means of production such as factories or equipment as the individual accumulates one's own surplus value that can be exchanged for a wage. Human capital's level of analysis is limited to the individual.

Cultural capital (Bourdieu, 1986) represents the investments of the dominant class in reproducing a set of symbols and meanings that give members a higher status in society. For example, dominant class parents provide their children with cultural capital by transmitting the attitudes and knowledge needed to succeed in the educational system. These symbols and attitudes are mostly transmitted inter-generationally within the dominant class but also can be acquired by the masses to a lesser degree. Cultural capital's level of analysis is extended to both the individual and class levels.

Along with classic, human, and cultural capital, social capital theory provides researchers with another lens through which to examine individuals' varying success in obtaining surplus value and returns. Social capital theory is increasingly a multidisciplinary concept, influential in the academic fields of economics, education, political science, public health, and organization studies. The theory's application to social, economic, and political problems generally yields a resounding conclusion: relationships matter. Adler and Kwon (2002) offer a general definition of social capital that resonates with how social capital is conceptualized across fields. They define social capital as the "goodwill that is engendered by the fabric of social relations and that can be mobilized to facilitate action" (p. 17).

Social capital is the investment in social networks as well as in mutual recognition and acknowledgment. Generally the more people one knows and the more one shares a common outlook with those acquaintances, the richer one is in social capital (Field, 2008). Implicit in these networks of social relations is the overall value to a network member. Knowing many people does not create quality social capital. Rather, quality social capital is dependent on the strength and quantity of human, cultural, economic, and social capital that individuals within a network possess and access over a lifetime (Kim & Schneider, 2005).

Social capital theory is one way to understand how individuals and networks interact within a specific social structure. The theory explores how individuals access resources through social relationships, and which types of relationships and resources are most conducive to building social capital. Therefore, the unit of analysis can be at both the individual and group levels. For the purposes of this study, I focus on the application of social capital theory to educational research and inquiry. Educational researchers are interested in applying the theory to understanding how individual students' social relationships and resources affect their academic trajectories within educational institutions.

Educational scholars have long documented how important quality sources of social capital are in students' academic success (Kao, 2004; Ream, 2005; Stanton-Salazar & Dornbusch, 1995; Teranishi & Briscoe, 2006). Reliable sources of social capital are particularly important to the academic success of those students who attend under-performing urban high schools (Tierney & Venegas, 2006). Students transitioning from secondary to postsecondary education often draw on different sources of social capital available at their schools and among their relatives and friends to successfully complete a college degree. For instance, a first-generation, low-income high school student wants to enroll at a four-year college immediately after high school. To accomplish this goal, the student needs to prepare for college admission while still in secondary school. The student cannot rely on relatives to provide timely and accurate college preparation information. Therefore, the student will rely on others—namely teachers, academic counselors, peers, and college preparation program personnel—for assistance in applying for college admission and financial aid. Each of these individuals represents a potential source of social capital that the student accesses while preparing for college enrollment. If the student cannot procure the necessary college preparation information from these individuals, the student will likely not be able to attend a four-year institution immediately after high school.

Accessing similar types of social capital is especially important for undocumented students. Undocumented students' unique financial, academic, and personal challenges to pursuing a postsecondary education require them to access even more specialized information for college preparation. They require long-lasting and reliable access to scarce and often clandestine information about in-state academic fee policies and undocumented-friendly scholarships and employment opportunities. Most undocumented students, as described in Chapter 4, rely on a variety of institutional agents, relatives, and peers for assistance in attending college. These sources of social capital are invaluable to their success in pursuing a postsecondary education, as the majority of undocumented students cannot attend college without others' continued support. Social capital theory is useful in chronicling how undocumented college students overcome recurring and significant obstacles in pursuing a postsecondary education. I now describe two distinct views of social capital as presented by Pierre Bourdieu and James Coleman. These two views dominate the social capital literature in the field of education and are pertinent to answering the study's research questions.

Pierre Bourdieu's "Bridging" Social Capital

Pierre Bourdieu became involved in social capital theory by way of his interest in the foundations of social order. As an extension of social order, Bourdieu found that economic, cultural, and social capital were grounded in the larger theories of social reproduction, and symbolic power and goods previously outlined by Karl Marx, Emile Durkheim, and Max Weber (Brubaker, 1985). Bourdieu (1986) defines social capital as "the aggregate of the actual or potential resources which are linked to possession of a durable network of more or less institutionalized relationships of mutual acquaintance and recognition" (p. 248). Membership in a particular network allows an individual to claim resources that are held collectively by the group. Bourdieu (1986) also explains that the size of the network determines the volume of social capital possessed by an individual. Further, the social obligations and connections contained within networks are at times convertible into economic capital.

According to Portes (1998), Bourdieu's concept of social capital can be reduced to two primary elements: (a) the social relationship that allows an individual to claim the resources of one's network associates, and (b) the quantity and quality of those network resources. It is through social capital that individuals have access to other types of capital—namely economic and cultural capital. These forms of capital aid the dominant class by maintaining and reproducing group solidarity, as well as exclusionary practices. In minimizing access to capital, the dominant class secures its commanding position within society (Lin, 1999; Portes, 1998).

Bourdieu (1986) describes three forms of cultural capital: embodied (long-lasting dispositions of the mind), objectified (cultural goods), and institutionalized (educational qualifications). Particular forms of cultural capital are more highly valued than others with each person bringing a particular *habitus*—a system of durable dispositions inculcated by objective structural conditions—to the field of interaction (Nash, 1999). Horvat (2001) explains that an individual's habitus reflects the internalization of structural boundaries and constraints, largely driving what an individual believes is possible and deserved. Hence, the powerful nature of cultural capital lies in the transmission, accumulation, and internalization of norms and expectations over one's entire socialization. Social capital, marked by its unspecified obligations and undetermined time horizons, fosters the transmission of cultural and economic capital resulting in access to powerful and enduring resources over a lifetime.

Bourdieu's (1986) concept of social capital requires a constant stream of interactions and exchanges on the part of network members. Further, he believes that social capital is an asset of the privileged classes in society (Field, 2008). Horvat (2001) explains that Bourdieu's sociology "aims at bridging the gap between individual action and social structure in shaping human interaction" (p. 200). In other words, social capital is just another apparatus of a larger social system of accessing resources and the reproduction of social class and stratification. This "bridging" view helps explain the varying levels of success among individuals as their actions can be facilitated by their direct and indirect links to others in their respective social networks (Adler & Kwon, 2002). The role of institutions of higher education facilitating the exchange and reproduction of social capital is of value in shaping policies and practices that provide opportunities for more diverse individuals to cultivate social capital.

The "bridging" version of social capital is useful in examining education-related issues as it provides a lens by which to explain differences in educational progress and attainment. Researchers can in part substantiate individual or group educational outcomes by looking at the quantity, quality, and frequency of their relationships and resources that foster academic goals inside and outside of school. Further, Bourdieu's version of social capital places the relationships and resources within a larger structural framework where individuals and groups have a relatively static place in society. This view is particularly helpful in studying the experiences of undocumented college students, as they are members of a larger hidden underclass in U.S. society. Navigating a postsecondary education without the formal and widespread recognition of institutional agents affects the quality and quantity of social capital available to undocumented students. I now turn to a description of another interpretation of social capital theory by James Coleman.

James Coleman's "Bonding" Social Capital
James Coleman, an American sociologist, came to contribute to social capital theory by way of his research on educational attainment in American communities. Unlike Bourdieu, Coleman strongly believes that social capital is not limited to the powerful in society (Field, 2008). Rather, individuals of all socioeconomic backgrounds access and build social capital during the course of their lives. Coleman (1990) states that social capital:

> constitutes a particular kind of resource available to an actor. Social capital is defined by its function. It is not a single entity but a variety of different entities, with two elements in common: they all consist of some aspect of social structures, and they facilitate certain actions of actors—whether persons or corporate actors—within the structure. (p. S98)

Coleman (1988) believes that social capital consists of norms and social control. Thus, social capital is intangible, embodied in the relations among people, and takes three primary forms: levels of trust as evidenced by obligations, expectations, and trustworthiness of structures; information channels; and norms and sanctions that promote the common good over self-interest (Coleman, 1988, 1990; Dika & Singh, 2002).

Coleman, like Bourdieu, emphasizes the importance of social networks in his version of social capital theory. An area of departure for Coleman (1988, 1990) is his particular attention to what he labels "intergenerational closure"—parents knowing the parents of their children's friends. Scholars believe that social closure is particularly important to social capital building in educational settings. For instance, the networks connecting the parents of adolescent classmates and friends facilitate effective norms like high school completion and college attendance (Dika & Singh, 2002; Horvat, Weininger, & Lareau, 2003). These effective norms facilitate or inhibit certain behaviors and actions, restricting an individual's actions for the sake of the public, communal good (Coleman, 1990). Putnam (1995) believes that organizations like the Parent Teacher Association (PTA) help build and sustain social capital in school settings. This type of organization ultimately contributes to the maintenance of civil engagement that benefits an entire society.

In comparison to Bourdieu's "bridging" social capital, Coleman's social capital is conceptualized as "bonding" (Adler & Kwon, 2002). Bonding focuses on the collectivity's characteristics and internal structure—the "linkages among individuals or groups within the collectivity and, specifically, in those features that give the collectivity cohesiveness and thereby facilitate the pursuit of collective goals" (Adler & Kwon, 2002, p. 21). Coleman (1990) also argues that structures, like voluntary organizations, produce both intentional and unintentional social capital. However, he is wary of what he sees as artificial social structures like government and corporate actors replacing primordial forms of social capital, since he believes the personal incentives to remain faithful to the unit disappear with individuals who are essentially "free riding" (p. 654). The forms of social capital that provide reciprocal benefits for a lifetime generally fall within family, clan, and community relationships. Hence it is the family's primary responsibility to adopt certain norms conducive to advancing their children's quality of life (Lareau, 2001).

Comparing bridging and bonding versions of social capital partly relies on contrasting the different types of relationships individuals and groups cultivate. Bridging social capital focuses on the external factors that constitute interpersonal relationships while bonding social capital focuses on the internal factors (Adler & Kwon, 2002; Tierney, 2006). On the one hand, external ties focusing on the bridging functions of social capital help explain the differential success of individuals and groups; success can be greatly facilitated by one's direct and indirect links to other actors in social networks. This perspective helps explain the benefits and opportunities an individual or group obtains as a result of membership in a reciprocal network. On the other hand, internal ties focusing on the bonding functions of social capital highlight the collective actors' internal characteristics; those internal features that give the network cohesiveness facilitate the pursuit of collective goals.

Another component of social capital that is useful in answering the study's research questions is the strength of social ties. The strength of these ties within an individual's or group's network dictates the type of resources accessed. Lin (1999), following the lead of Granovetter (1973, 1982), argues that the strength of ties—either strong or weak—serves different purposes. Strong ties are those relationships with family members and close friends with whom an individual shares high levels of intimacy and trust. In contract, weak ties are those relationships with acquaintances from different social and cultural backgrounds; these ties are found in low-density networks where individuals are less connected with each other. Lin argues that strong ties bring together individuals and groups with similar resources in order to pursue expressive purposes—normative and identity-based goals (Field, 2008). Weak ties serve instrumental goals since they provide access to new types of people and resources that rely less on strongly-shared values. Thus, strong and weak ties provide distinct advantages in accomplishing different goals.

Relating Social Capital to Undocumented Student Experiences
As I discuss in Chapters 4 and 5, informants did not always exclusively develop bridging or bonding social capital. For instance, a student may have participated in a campus undocumented support group that provided access to an entire network of undocumented-friendly advocates and organizations that assisted her in securing financing for college (bridging social capital). That same student's parents may have purposively moved to a school district with a higher college attendance record, thus creating an environment and expectation of postsecondary attendance (bonding social capital). In this case, the student benefited from both bridging and bonding social capital. Also, individual students relied on internal and external factors during their social capital building. At times students benefitted from strong ties while at other times they were better served by transitory weak ties. In this study, I consider various manifestations of social capital to be beneficial to an undocumented student's postsecondary academic success.

No known studies have explicitly employed the social capital theoretical framework to understand the experiences of undocumented students. Research with students has primarily focused on their academic resiliency (Perez et al., 2009), the community cultural wealth students bring with them to educational settings (Perez Huber, 2009), or the impact of undocumented-friendly legislation on students' college attendance (Abrego, 2006, 2008; Flores, 2010; Flores & Horn, 2009; Flores & Oseguera, 2009). Other studies have focused on the impact of being undocumented on students' academic trajectories (Gonzales, 2009; Perez, 2009) or how the media portrays undocumented student issues (Jefferies, 2009). As the literature on undocumented college students has grown, researchers have pursued the subject from various angles following no single research agenda or theme. This study attempts to take another angle—how students access social capital in lieu of traditional forms of economic, human, and cultural capital in completing a postsecondary education.

This study utilizes elements of both Bourdieu's and Coleman's visions of social capital. An examination of undocumented student experiences benefits from both theorists since Bourdieu focuses on class agency while Coleman focuses on individual agency (Musoba & Baez, 2009). Both types of agency are pertinent to the experiences of an individual undocumented college student who inhabits a distinct social underclass. This structure/agency dichotomy may manifest in the creation of a communal and/or personal college-going identity contrary to the dominant social and political influences that discourage and invalidate such actions. On the one hand, an undocumented college student makes a conscious decision to pursue a postsecondary education even though most social, economic, and cultural indicators suggest it is a poor decision riddled with opportunities to be exposed by immigration authorities (Negron-Gonzalez, 2009). On the other hand, an undocumented college student who keeps his immigration status secret out of fear of legal repercussions maintains a sense of social respect and legitimacy by pursuing a postsecondary education. This study chronicles such realities and how they impact students' abilities to successfully earn a bachelor's degree.

Bourdieu's and Coleman's views of social capital are also useful to this study since they respectively focus on external and internal ties (Adler & Kwon, 2002; Tierney, 2006). The external perspective highlights the importance of institutional agents knowing about undocumented students' needs. If agents are aware of students' realities, they can positively influence policy that affects this largely invisible group of students. The internal perspective helps explain the benefits and opportunities undocumented students obtain when they join an on-campus student support group that provides them with a forum to discuss their educational goals and a pool of resources to help realize those goals. Undocumented college students' academic trajectories are driven by the external and internal ties that they have with institutional agents, benefactors, undocumented-friendly support groups, and friends and family.

Considerations When Applying Social Theory
While social capital theory has been widely used in educational studies as a means to explain differences in educational attainment, there are also some noteworthy criticisms to keep in mind when it is applied to an investigation of undocumented college students. One serious weakness is the original conceptualization of social capital by Coleman in 1990 (Morrow, 1999; Portes, 1998, 2000). Critics point to the fact that his conceptualization is much too vague to develop testable hypotheses. Further, Coleman's social capital relies on a top-down view of the parent-child relationship leaving little to no opportunity for the agency of adolescents in accessing social capital on their own; all social capital is accessed via a parent in an intact, traditional family structure. This scenario is not always present in the case of the nine students profiled in this study.

The same vagueness that applies to Coleman's conceptualization can be found in Bourdieu's (1986) theoretical version. Musoba and Baez (2009) point to the fact that social capital is often over-simplified. In particular, the uncritical use of Bourdieu's bridging social capital can result in a masking of class struggles. Further, Coleman's version of social capital largely ignores the oppressive aspect of social relations on which bonding social capital is centered. Coleman speaks to the individual mobility associated with social capital but fails to "account for the roles it plays in the social processes which will continue to demand that individuals own this or that kind of capital in order to be deemed worthy of the social resources invested in them" (Musoba & Baez, p. 168). These criticisms are relevant to this study as undocumented immigrants are members of a distinct underclass that is illegally present in the US. Applying social capital theory to a study of undocumented students without considering the practical ramifications of their belonging to a largely disenfranchised underclass could lead to a further simplification of their educational experiences.

Another weakness of social capital theory is its reliance on the resources inherent in the structure of relationships. According to Portes and Landolt (1996), this reliance leads to two conceptual issues. First, the sources of social capital—namely relationships—are confused with the benefits derived from it, leading to a circular reasoning because the presence of social capital is often inferred from the assets that an individual or group acquires. For example, a student who secures the money necessary to pay for college from one's relatives is thought to have social capital, whereas a student who does not secure the money has no social capital. Such an inference does not take into account the possibility that the unsuccessful student also may have highly supportive social networks that simply lack the economic means to meet such an expense. The second issue is that the disentanglement of the possession of social capital from its activation becomes nearly impossible (Dika & Singh, 2002). It becomes difficult to distinguish between the ability to access social capital and the ability to activate it resulting in a desirable outcome. As described in Chapter 4, issues of benefits and disentanglement are constantly present in students' lives. Distinguishing between genuine sources of social capital and unintentional circumstances is important to keep in mind throughout the study.

Academics most critical of social capital theory also focus on its shortcomings in explaining how race, ethnicity, and class affect its development and application (Dika & Singh, 2002; Lareau & Horvat, 1999; Stanton-Salazar, 1997; Stanton-Salazar & Dornbusch, 1995). Stanton-Salazar and Dornbusch (1995) argue that supportive ties with institutional agents vary between solid middle-class students and Mexican-origin high school students. Therefore, they advocate for an alternative social reproduction theory that is inclusive of the realities of ethnic minorities. Stanton-Salazar (1997) outlines the specific institutional and ideological forces that make access to social capital and institutional support within educational settings so difficult for working-class minority students. These studies question social capital as a catchall for the positive effects of sociability, without consideration of evidence that shows how race, ethnicity, and class have a negative influence on traditional social capital acquisition. Again an examination of racial and ethnic minorities, such as this study attempts, needs to regularly account for these negative influences.

There are other specific drawbacks of applying social capital theory to studying undocumented college students. Prolonged engagement with these students in order to identify and understand the available forms of social capital within their networks is challenging given the economic, educational, and social circumstances caused by their immigration status. Further, because there are so many limitations placed on undocumented college students' access to financial aid and college services, distinguishing the difference between the possession of social capital from its activation becomes challenging. For instance, there is no way to know if students could activate certain types of social capital since they may be barred from accessing a counseling or tutoring program due to lack of residency or official financial aid eligibility. There are also ethical considerations for the application of social capital theory to studying undocumented students. As social networks are difficult to navigate as an outsider, adding another layer—undocumented immigration status—to an already complex composition of racial, ethnic, and socioeconomic factors may be too overwhelming to identify and document in the course of a research project.

TYING SOCIAL CAPITAL TO THE RESEARCH QUESTIONS

Before moving on to the methodological framework for this study, I want to revisit the four research questions that guide this study:

1. How do undocumented college students develop, maintain, and exchange social capital?
2. Do the social support networks of undocumented college students factor into educational outcomes?
3. How do experiences of exclusion shape the educational identity and consciousness of undocumented students?
4. How do the contours of an undocumented student's identity enable or disable academic performance?

These four questions are a starting point from which I can understand how the acquisition and application of social capital affects undocumented students' postsecondary goals. I aim to describe how individuals learn about the limitations posed by their immigration status and how they react to the obstacles. Using social capital theory, I want to chronicle who helps students prepare for and transition to college. I also want to explain how individuals and social support networks may or may not be successful in procuring relevant and useful sources of social capital. I intend to describe how individual agency helps students overcome structural barriers to a postsecondary education. Finally, I want to understand how different types of social capital revealed in networks and relationships best serve students' interests at various times in their educational careers.

Undocumented students make sense of their immigration status and its respective limitations by observing relatives, friends, and peers that share the same circumstances. Students look to institutional agents such as instructors, counselors, and mentors for direction and support in navigating their postsecondary education goals. They also rely on their individual abilities to attend college while fulfilling their other familial and personal responsibilities. Social capital theory provides a tool by which to respond to these realities and experiences. By employing the theory as my interpretive lens for analyzing the experiences of undocumented students, I may come to better understand the distinct factors that allow students to pursue a postsecondary education. I now turn to a discussion of method.

CHAPTER THREE

Research Design and Method

I walked up to the table in the breezeway. The Metropolitan University (Metro U.) undocumented student club—IMAGINE—was hosting a fundraiser bake sale that day. They had set out a table in their usual spot to sell coffee, soft drinks, candy, baked goods, and tamales. The students working the table smiled at me while I surveyed my options. One of the younger students approached and asked me what I wanted. She addressed me by my name. "I'll have a coffee and sweet tamale, please." She was putting together my order when I introduced myself to her. "We haven't met but I'm Lisa. What's your name?" She responded shyly, "It's Alba." I asked Alba how she knew my name. I had seen her before at a few of the IMAGINE meetings but I had never talked to her. She explained, "I've seen you at the meetings. You sort of stick out so I remembered your name." I chuckled. "What do you mean I stick out?" Alba blushed. "Well, you know … you look different than us. It's hard not to notice you." I smiled and nodded my head. She handed me the tamale and coffee and I thanked her.

I found a seat in the courtyard and enjoyed my food and drink. I had a clear view of the bake sale and I took inventory of the students working the table. Alba was right—I did look different than the club members. Not only was I about 10 years older than most of the students, I was also taller than them and I was the only one with blonde hair. As a nonimmigrant studying undocumented immigrants, my appearance, attitudes and beliefs, and objectives as a researcher were of concern to the research informants. Many students assumed that I was married since my surname is Garcia. Some students asked me why I did not speak fluent Spanish since my father's family is from Mexico. Others questioned why I was interested in the topic of undocumented immigration since I was not an immigrant myself. A few shared with me that I was the first Caucasian-looking person with whom they had ever shared their status. Students questioned me about my motives before we started interviews or observations. Others inquired about my personal life and experiences when I spent the day with them or mingled with them at events.

The researcher/informant dynamic as well as the study population required me to constantly reflect on both the nature of this study and its effects on the informants. Given the sensitive nature of navigating life as an adult undocumented immigrant, it was important for me to think carefully about how to approach this research project from beginning to end. In the discussion that follows, I review how I conducted research on undocumented college students. I begin by restating the research questions that guided this study. Next, I provide an overview of my research design as well as describe the process of identifying and recruiting students. I explain the three methods used to collect data: observations, interviews, and document analysis. I then detail the procedures used for data analysis and discuss how I ensured trustworthiness throughout the research process. Finally, I end with a brief discussion about the theoretical perspective that influenced my position as a researcher.

RESEARCH DESIGN

Undocumented college students and their educational experiences have been minimally studied using both quantitative and qualitative studies. Quantitative studies of undocumented students highlight the persistence and academic resilience of students (e.g., Flores, 2010; Flores & Chapa, 2009; Flores & Horn, 2009; Perez et al., 2009). While such studies are useful in painting broad strokes of undocumented college student experiences, they do not provide the details about how matriculation actually occurs. Other scholars (e.g., Abrego, 2006, 2008; Gildersleeve, 2010; Gonzales, 2007, 2009; Perez, 2009; Perez Huber, 2009) have conducted qualitative interviews and observations, seeking to understand students' experiences living in the shadows of society while simultaneously pursuing postsecondary education goals. These accounts provide a more nuanced description of undocumented students' experiences.

Answering my research questions required utilizing a methodological approach to inquiry that provided the ability to not only look at my subjects' experiences during the time I spent with them, but also gain insight about their previous life and educational experiences. I also wanted a methodological approach that allowed for insight into students' future employment and educational prospects. For undocumented students, matriculating to a four-year institution was not simply a matter of meeting admission eligibility requirements, applying to college, and then enrolling in classes. Rather, these students followed a trajectory infused with limitations and experiences unique only to undocumented immigrants. They drew from both their past and present experiences of exclusion and inclusion as well as their anticipation of being college educated for motivation and direction. Thus, their college-going experiences were always rooted in the past, present, and future.

Given this study's research questions and the challenges undocumented postsecondary students encounter, I chose to employ qualitative methods as quantitative methods would not provide me with the answers I sought. Denzin and Lincoln (2000) explain that qualitative researchers emphasize the value-laden nature of inquiry; researchers seek answers to questions that explain how social experience is created and given meaning. This qualitative study focused on the educational experiences and perceptions of undocumented college students currently attending Metro. U. Further, it focused on how these students construct and enact their identities as college students in complex learning and living environments that simultaneously discourage and encourage their presence and participation.

THE CASE FOR QUALITATIVE METHODOLOGY
A qualitative researcher's primary goal is to create and bring psychological and emotional unity to an interpretive experience (Denzin & Lincoln, 2000). This is accomplished by employing those methods that are conducive to fostering an interactive research process. To understand the experiences of undocumented college students and the way in which they make meaning of their past and present interactions, I took a qualitative approach to this study.

In this study, I was interested in learning how undocumented college students develop college-going identities as well as how they persisted in pursuing their postsecondary goals. As a nonimmigrant outsider observing these students, I felt that I might be more able to identify how the students successfully navigated the college-going process. Understanding meaning necessitates that the researcher interact with participants, preferably on an in-depth basis over a period of time. Qualitative researchers draw upon multiple methods, including observations and interviews, to conduct their research. They spend adequate time with the subjects to gain a fuller understanding of the subjects and collected data (Creswell, 2007). Spending time with subjects requires the researcher to acknowledge one's own positions, perceptions, and biases (Fine & Weis, 1996). Important in this qualitative study was also the vulnerable nature of undocumented students. The students' vulnerability was a constant issue in the planning and execution of the study's data collection. For instance, I acknowledged early on that campus and community gatekeepers would be instrumental in both identifying study participants and establishing credibility as a legitimate researcher among undocumented students (Fine & Weis, 1996; Fine, Weis, Weseen, & Wong, 2000; Weis & Fine, 2000). I also had to be sensitive to the research limitations set by the Institutional Review Boards (IRB) at both my institution and Metro U. I was mindful of the limited time I had to collect data, as many of the students would either finish their degrees by the end of the year or take anticipated breaks in enrollment due to financial issues. Thus, I conducted intense and repeated observations and individual interviews over the course of the 2009–2010 academic year at Metro U. and select University of California (UC) and California State University (CSU) campuses.

Entry and Site Selection
This study drew upon various qualitative research methods to investigate the experiences of undocumented postsecondary students attending four-year institutions. Identifying undocumented students posed a significant obstacle during all stages of data collection. Many institutions as well as large postsecondary systems and states do not track the size of their undocumented student populations (Batalova & Fix, 2006; Passel, 2003). Some universities publish annual reports estimating the numbers of their potential undocumented students while others are just beginning to collect undocumented student data (Blackburn, 2009; University of California, 2010).

My primary data collection location—Metro U.—neither collected nor published an official report on the exact number of undocumented immigrants matriculating on campus. Therefore, I could not approach the administration for a roster of enrolled undocumented students. Further, due to confidentiality issues related to the study population, approaching individual institutional agents regarding the whereabouts of students was also not an option. Site selection had to be strategic so as to maximize both the number of matriculating undocumented students and the probability of securing the participation of informants through snowball sampling (Salganik & Heckathorn, 2004; Watters & Biernacki, 1989). My goal was to recruit approximately 25 current undocumented Metro U. students for the study.

Metro U. is a large, public, comprehensive university situated at the heart of a vast metropolitan area. It is one of the 23 campuses that constitute the CSU. The university enrolls approximately 20,000 students; 75% of the students are undergraduates and 60% are women. Approximately 37% of the students attend Metro U. on a part-time basis. Metro U. is a Hispanic-Serving Institution (HSI) with 55% of the student body being Latino, 22% Asian, 15% White, and 8% African American. Almost 80% of Metro U.'s student body hails from the surrounding metropolitan area. The university's academic fees totaled approximately $4,893 for academic year 2009–2010.

Metro U.'s demographics, location, and academic fees provided a sound justification for its selection as a primary study location. The university's overwhelming Latino majority made it a more desirable place to locate undocumented students since 76% of the nation's undocumented population is Hispanic (Passel & Cohn, 2009). Further, Metro U. is located in the same metropolitan area that is home to the largest undocumented immigrant population in the nation (Hill & Hayes, 2013). It is assumed that because of the sizeable undocumented population, area postsecondary institutions will likely enroll relatively significant numbers of undocumented students since they will be able to save money by commuting from home. Since undocumented students are not eligible for state and federal financial aid, Metro U.'s relatively low academic fees also makes it a more desirable institution for enrollment.

Finally, I chose Metro U. as the primary research location since I had longstanding connections with Metro U. students due to previous research conducted at the location (Garcia & Tierney, 2011). Establishing relationships with vulnerable and hidden populations requires negotiating with gatekeepers whom informants know and trust (Tierney & Hallett, 2010). As with most research concerning hidden or vulnerable populations, access to sites often begins with gatekeepers who hold insider status within the population (Creswell, 2007). My relationship with recent Metro U. graduates facilitated introductions to current Metro U. undocumented students. I then used these new relationships with current Metro U. students to meet more undocumented students on campus. This snowball sampling technique (Salganik & Heckathorn, 2004) facilitated introductions to campus undocumented students throughout the academic year. I was also able to gain access to the weekly meetings of the campus undocumented student group—IMAGINE. At these meetings, I interacted with students and established my status as a legitimate, trustworthy researcher. Subsequent group fundraisers, activities, and events further allowed me to introduce myself to undocumented students.

Participant Selection

The first step in participant selection was to secure permission from the Institutional Review Board (IRB) at both my institution and Metro U. Once I received permission from both campus IRB offices, I began recruiting study participants. There were three criteria used to determine eligibility for the study. All student informants had to be: (a) currently undocumented immigrants, (b) age 18 or older, and (c) currently attending Metro U. I provided students with the IRB-approved study recruitment flyer (see Appendix A) as well as my professional business card containing both my mobile phone number and university e-mail address. The flyer included information about what participation in the study would entail and asked the students to contact me if they were interested in participating. I met the majority of Metro U. participants through undocumented student acquaintances and at weekly IMAGINE meetings and events.

Most students that I approached were receptive to participating in the study. This was largely due to my existing relationships with Metro U. undocumented student leaders. I also benefitted from using snowball sampling—a process by which I routinely asked study participants to refer me to other undocumented students who may want to participate in the study. Once a student agreed to participate, we then scheduled an interview at a convenient time and place. All student interviews were individually scheduled due to IRB-established guidelines regarding confidentiality. Before interviews began, I reviewed with the informants all of the detailed information on the IRB-approved study information sheet (see Appendix B). I answered all of the participants' questions and encouraged them to contact me at any point after the interview if they had any further questions or concerns. Due to the nature of the subject population, both campus IRB offices determined that written consent was optional. Students could consent by way of answering the interview questions. I used an IRB-approved interview protocol (see Appendix C) for all formal interviews. As expected in any qualitative study, additional questions arose during the course of the research. For secondary interviews and/or observations, I did not use a protocol.

A total of 25 Metro U. students participated in semi-structured in-depth interviews during the 2009–2010 academic year (see Table 1). Participants in this study included undergraduates of every level from a variety of academic disciplines. Among the 25 students, two students were working on post-baccalaureate teaching credentials and one was completing a master's degree. Although the university serves a large population of non-Latino students, all of the Metro U. undocumented student participants were Mexican nationals. Participants included 16 women and nine men, all between the age of 18 and 30. Of the 25 participants, nine students were asked to participate in follow-up interviews and observations based on their availability. Detailed summaries of the nine students are provided in Chapter 4.

In addition to interviewing and observing Metro U. students, I also conducted supplementary interviews with 15 undocumented students attending UC and CSU campuses throughout California (see Table 2). These students were also contacted for their participation in the study via snowball sampling using pre-existing contacts in the undocumented student community. All 15 students were undergraduates ranging from age 18 to 24; eleven were female, three were male, and one was transgender. Again, all participating students were Latino, originating from El Salvador, Guatemala, and Mexico. I used the same IRB-approved recruitment flyer, study information sheet, and interview protocol when recruiting and interviewing this smaller group of research informants (see Appendices A, B, and C).

Table 1. Metropolitan University Student Characteristics

Name	Age	Sex	Age of Arrival	Level	Major
Abel	24	M	6	Senior	Criminal Justice
Alba	18	F	7	Frosh	Undecided
Alberto	21	M	12	Junior	Math
Alejandra	20	F	8 mos.	Junior	Social work
Alex	23	M	4	Senior	Business Admin.
Blanca	20	F	9	Junior	Political Science
Cristina	20	F	3 mos.	Junior	Spanish
Jackie	23	F	3	Senior	Political Science
Janelle	24	F	5	Junior	Political Science
Julia	18	F	13	Frosh	Undecided
Luis	20	M	4	Junior	Biology
Luz	20	F	13	Junior	Sociology
Manny	19	M	6	Soph.	Computer Science
Marcos	26	M	15	Senior	Marketing
Marina	24	F	2	Senior	Psychology
Marissa	25	F	6	Graduate	Social Work
Monica	22	F	11	Junior	Sociology
Paloma	21	F	11 mos.	Soph.	Undecided
Ramona	19	F	6 mos.	Soph.	Special Education
Ricky	22	M	7	Senior	Computer Animation
Roberto	24	M	14	Senior	Latin American Studies
Romero	30	M	11	Post-Bac	Teaching Credential
Sara	23	F	14	Post-Bac	Teaching Credential
Stephanie	20	F	2	Junior	Political Science
Tesla	22	F	11	Senior	Sociology

Table 2. UC and CSU Student Characteristics

Name	Age	Sex	Country of Origin	Age of Arrival	Level	Major
Abigail	20	F	Mexico	10	Junior	Development Studies
Belen	19	F	Mexico	8 mos.	Frosh	Aerospace Engineering
Benito	20	M	Mexico	16	Frosh	Undecided
Betty	19	F	El Salvador	16	Soph.	Ethnic Studies
Camila	21	F	Mexico	6	Junior	Human Services
Chavela	20	F	El Salvador	3	Soph.	Political Science
Daniela	22	F	Mexico	5	Senior	Mathematics
Fabian	21	M	Mexico	6	Junior	Anthropology
Fidel	19	M	Mexico	9	Soph.	Mathematics
Juana	19	F	Mexico	7	Frosh	Biochemistry
Linda	20	F	Mexico	2	Senior	Ethnic Studies
Pia	20	F	Guatemala	15	Frosh	Biology
Rosita	19	F	Mexico	9 mos.	Frosh	Undecided
Sol	24	T	Mexico	3	Senior	Community Studies
Tamar	20	F	Mexico	2	Junior	Gender Studies

RESEARCH METHOD

This study draws upon three methods—participant observations, interviews, and document analysis—to understand how undocumented students create personal and communal identities that foster the development of class-based social capital that in turn helps them attend four-year institutions.

Observations

Observations of the students and related campus and community activities were conducted throughout the project. Observation research typically occurs in a natural context. Adler and Adler (1994) explain that during observation, "behavior and interaction continue as they would without the presence of a researcher" (p. 378). Observation requires that researchers enter the field for a prolonged period of time to observe and occasionally interact with study participants (Bogdan & Taylor, 1975). Observers may take on a variety of roles, ranging from passive observer to active participant. Angrosino and Mays de Perez (2000) argue that researchers do not step into defined positions. Rather, they negotiate with participants to determine the type of role they might assume during the research project. Observation was a particularly useful tool for studying undocumented students since it allowed me to experience the ways in which students' immigration statuses influenced their academic behavior and actions.

Atkinson and Hammersley (1994) explain that participant observation "rests on the principle of interaction and the 'reciprocity of perspectives' between social actors" (p. 256). This egalitarian position is based on the notion that both the observer and the observed are different but equal. Acknowledging both my privilege as an observer and as a U.S. citizen was key to building trust with student informants. I discussed with students that my observations of them were to be treated as a dialogue between two strangers getting acquainted with one another (Tyler, 1986). This open dialogue provoked both questions and requests from informants. They often inquired about what I thought about the classes they attended or the quality of their neighborhood schools. Some asked me about why I chose to enroll in graduate school. On occasion I was asked to elaborate on education-related issues during IMAGINE meetings. One student even asked me if I could borrow a book from my own university library so she did not have to purchase it herself. Their inquiries about my own perspectives and resources solidified our relationship as co-observers; they observed me as much as I observed them.

Observations provided me the opportunity to view undocumented students' experiences as both insider and outsider simultaneously (Spradley, 1980). Researchers often balance two very different tasks as both an insider and outsider; they have to adopt the perspectives of participants while simultaneously trying to remain detached in order to facilitate data collection and analysis (Bogdan & Biklen, 1992; Bogdan & Taylor, 1975). I gained the trust of the informants by consistently attending the weekly IMAGINE meetings as well as selected campus and community events sponsored by other immigrant rights groups and IMAGINE. I attended IMAGINE fundraisers, a campus and statewide budget cuts protest in which IMAGINE students participated, as well as immigrant messaging training sessions and community informational sessions. I also accompanied individual students to their places of employment, spent time with them in their homes, and interacted with their parents and siblings. I met students' significant others and was invited to birthday parties, holiday gatherings, and graduation celebrations.

For this study, I engaged in two types of participant observations—group and individual. Group observations started in September 2009 and continued through June 2010. These observations included meetings or gatherings where Metro U. undocumented students congregated. I attended weekly IMAGINE meetings including most of their fundraisers, community outreach events, and campus information sessions. These observations provided detailed insight into how the students as a group went about attending college as undocumented immigrants. I witnessed how they fundraised for their operating and scholarship funds as well as how they used the proceeds to design outreach programs targeting the greater campus community and local high schools. Group observations also allowed me to document how Metro U. undocumented students gathered information beneficial to college attendance such as scholarship, employment, and campus leadership opportunities.

I also engaged in individual observations throughout the study (see Table 3). As I discuss in Chapter 4, I observed nine individual Metro U. students for a day at a time. Depending on the availability of the individual students, I usually met students at the beginning of the day and followed them for as long as possible. I accompanied them on their commutes to campus as well as attended classes with them. I went to two students' places of employment for a day. I even visited some students' homes, enabling me to interact with their parents, siblings, and other relatives. These types of individual observations provided insight into the day-to-day activities of undocumented students. I was able to gain a deeper understanding of just how typical and atypical their days could be as undocumented immigrants. For example, by riding public transportation with students to and from school, I was able to understand how a 30-minute one-way commute by car could take three or four times longer due to a student not being able to secure a driver's license because of one's immigration status.

Table 3. Observation Details

Observed	Type	Duration	Location	Frequency
IMAGINE meetings	Group	1–1.5 hrs.	On-campus locations	17
IMAGINE-sponsored events (e.g., high school presentations, fundraisers, open houses, outreach events, social gatherings)	Group	1–4 hrs.	On- and off-campus locations	14
Education budget cuts action day protest	Group	Full day	On- and off-campus locations	1
Immigrant rights community events	Group	1–3 hrs.	On- and off-campus locations	3
Metro U. students	Individual	1–1.5 hrs.	On- and off-campus locations	25
Metro U. profiled students	Individual	Full day	On- and off-campus locations	9

Following each observation, I wrote a summary of the day's events, including location and time, persons present, events observed, and emergent themes. I kept a diary on hand during all observations so as to take notes. During club meetings or class observations, I was able to take more complete notes. In those circumstances when taking copious notes was inappropriate, I jotted down key words in my diary or left notes on my digital voice recorder during breaks. This was more common when I was mingling with students, attending fundraisers, or visiting them at their homes. I completed my summaries immediately after leaving the field to maximize the amount of information I was able to recall.

Interviews

Throughout the project I conducted formal and informal qualitative interviews. Kvale (2007) explains that an interview is part of the common culture of the age. The interview is "a conversation that has a structure and a purpose determined by ... the interviewer" (p. 7). An interview is usually semi-structured, with a particular sequence of themes to be covered as well as some prepared questions. Qualitative interviews are not wholly spontaneous but are purposeful in their planning and execution. Researchers are required to carefully listen and strategically respond so as to evoke both meaningful questions and answers from informants (Spradley, 1979).

Interviews allowed me to probe students about their individual and group circumstances and experiences. As with observations, interviews can be significantly influenced by the relationship between the interviewer and participants. Fontana and Frey (2000) suggest that "interviews are interactional encounters and ... the nature of the social dynamic of the interview can shape the nature of the knowledge generated" (p. 647). Each participant responds to an interviewer differently; some may feel more comfortable and will share more information whereas others may feel intimidated and give abbreviated responses. Building rapport—a harmonious relationship between researcher and informant (Creswell, 2007; Spradley, 1979)—is necessary in facilitating an interview that best describes informants' experiences. Rapport facilitates and enhances a researcher's ability to elicit information from a culture-sharing group that is useful in later description and analysis (Spradley, 1979). For instance, some of the informants in this study were excited to participate in further interviews and observations since the primary interview had uncovered truths and experiences they had not previously considered important to their development as undocumented students. In these cases, students were eager to help me document the life-altering experiences that they did not previously recognize or value.

I conducted two types of interviews—formal and informal—throughout the course of the study. I conducted formal interviews with 25 Metro U. students using a formal semi-structured interview protocol—a set of questions to guide the interview but allowing the participant more of a role in shaping the interview's direction (see Appendix C). I formally interviewed each study informant one time during data collection. These interviews took place between November

2009 and June 2010. On average, interviews lasted approximately one hour and took place at the convenience of participants either on or off campus. Most interviewees chose to be interviewed on the Metro U. campus, as it was the most convenient place for them to meet. There were some students that asked to be interviewed at locations in their own neighborhoods since it was more convenient or because they preferred to not run into classmates or campus acquaintances during the interview.

Informal interviews were also conducted from September 2009 through June 2010. These interviews mostly took place during group and individual observations and did not follow any structured interview protocol. Informal interviews allowed for follow-up and clarification of data collected during observations and formal interviews. I also used informal interviews as a means by which to stay up-to-date on current campus and community events. During both types of interviews, student informants were encouraged to engage in a dialogue with me, including asking me questions and sharing concerns about the research project and its objectives.

All interviewees agreed to be digitally recorded during their formal interviews. I personally transcribed all interviews. During each formal interview, I took brief notes about the interview setting as well as the interviewee. During informal interviews, I jotted down notes or recorded notes using a digital tape recorder. I produced a one-page interview summary for each interview including emerging themes and possible follow-up questions and topics for future meetings and observations. Since I had weekly contact with many of the research informants, I could relatively quickly clarify questions or concerns after transcription. This process facilitated the final data analysis of the project.

Supplementary interviews
Throughout the course of the study, I conducted supplemental interviews with an additional 15 undocumented students attending UC and CSU campuses. These students were selected via snowball sampling using preexisting contacts in the undocumented student community. Supplemental interviews were used in two primary ways. First, the majority of these interviews provided more information about how undocumented students pursued their postsecondary goals in different educational settings. This was particularly relevant to those

students attending the UC. For instance, UC undocumented students attended a significantly more competitive and selective institution than Metro U. Also students paid higher academic fees in the amount of $9,311—almost double the amount paid by Metro U. students. Finally, another significant difference between UC and Metro U. students was that the majority of UC students lived far from home. As a result, most of them did not live with their families and often incurred much higher living expenses associated with residing in on- or off-campus housing.

The second way in which these interviews were useful was that the conversations provided more insight about the general awareness undocumented students had about policies, practices, and opportunities that enabled them to pursue a postsecondary education. For the supplemental interviews, campus gatekeepers were contacted in advance of my visit. I then made individual arrangements with those students who expressed interest in participating in the study. Participants felt comfortable to discuss their ideas freely in a confidential atmosphere. Each interview lasted approximately one hour and was recorded and transcribed for analysis. Supplemental interviews were an additional way to obtain trustworthy contextual data that was useful in final data analysis.

Document Analysis
Although observations and interviews composed the majority of data I collected, I also engaged in document analysis (see Table 4). I started collecting and reviewing documents in January 2009. I joined the mailing lists of research centers such as the Migration Policy Institute, the Pew Hispanic Center, and the Center for the Study of Immigrant Integration so as to stay current with policies and research on the subject. I also regularly reviewed news outlets such as the *Los Angeles Times*, *New York Times*, *The Sacramento Bee*, and *San Francisco Chronicle* for immigration-related stories. I paid particular attention to those issues concerning undocumented immigrants and their intersection with K–12 education, higher education, and employment issues. I also reviewed relevant academic news outlets—*The Chronicle of Higher Education, Inside Higher Ed*, and the *Education Commission of the States E-Clips*—for undocumented immigrant-related stories, especially the most recent state and national challenges and amendments to legislation that impact college students.

Table 4. Research Methods Used

Method	Targeted Group	Duration	Frequency	Timeline
Observation (group and individual)	Metro U. students	Varied	Averaged several group and individual observations per week	Sept. 2009– June 2010
Interviews (formal)	Metro U. students	1–1.5 hrs.	25	Nov. 2009– June 2010
Interviews (formal)	UC and CSU students	1–1.5 hrs.	15	Nov. 2009– June 2010
Interviews (informal)	Metro U. students	Varied	Averaged several per week	Sept. 2009– June 2010
Document analysis	News outlets; IMAGINE discussion board; social networking sites; e-mails	Varied	Averaged several per week	Jan. 2009– June 2010

Another source of document analysis available to me during this study was the IMAGINE discussion board. I relied on the board to stay current with all of Metro U.'s undocumented student activities, events, fundraisers, and scholarships. Members of the discussion group regularly posted employment, volunteer, and political organizing opportunities available to undocumented immigrants. I reviewed all of these posts, including IMAGINE's printed and video recruitment materials, during data analysis.

Finally, I joined available undocumented student groups and forums on social networking sites like Facebook to stay current with issues and activities. Analysis of Facebook and group posts was used to frame the study and identify issues within Metro U.'s undocumented community. I was able to track the planning and development of several fundraising and political action projects students participated in by reviewing e-mails and Facebook messages. I was also able to keep in touch with students who were unable to enroll for a term due to financial hardships. Table 4 summarizes the methods used, the frequency in which they were employed, and the timeline for data collection.

Exiting the Research Process

Primary data collection for this study began in September 2009 and ended in June 2010. The relationships that developed between a few of the study participants and me continued past the end of data collection and analysis. I remained in contact with some of the students through social networking websites and e-mail. Some students continued to invite me to undocumented immigrant events and fundraisers. I also remained a member of the IMAGINE discussion board so that I could stay current on events and issues. As some of the students were graduating from Metro U. during the 2009–2010 academic year, I was also invited to the IMAGINE graduation celebration for family and friends. Students would periodically contact me for current information about undocumented students for class projects and assignments. They also contacted me to see how my study was progressing and ask for general advice about enrolling in graduate school.

Data Analysis

Throughout data analysis, my primary goal was to find connections between the environments undocumented immigrant students inhabited and how individual and group experiences shaped students' college-going attitudes and actions. By comparing common themes found in the collected observations, interviews, and documents, an image of students' college-going experiences emerged. So as to familiarize myself with the data as best I could, I personally transcribed all of the recorded interviews. I also re-wrote all of my observation and field notes. I utilized Atlas.ti, a qualitative data analysis software, to organize and code all of the data in one location on my computer. Atlas.ti provides the tools to help the researcher concisely analyze the data; the program does not analyze the data according to a preconceived script or program.

I relied on the constant comparative method (CCM) for all data analysis. CCM enables the researcher to collect and analyze data simultaneously (Boeije, 2002; Glaser & Strauss, 1967). After the collection of an initial set of data, I identified codes and themes that emerged. At this stage, I had identified approximately 20 preliminary codes. These codes included both descriptive and explanatory categories that allowed me to think more critically of the data (Lincoln & Guba, 1985). I set these preliminary codes aside and continued collecting data.

After I collected more data, I repeated the coding process. This time, I coded data in relation to previously collected data. I collapsed and re-worked most of the codes so as to better organize the data. This continual redefining of categories and criteria rendered the original codes as general and contingent, far from final themes I anticipated producing at the end of the project (Dye, Schatz, Rosenberg, & Coleman, 2000). I continued this process several times throughout the study. The goal was to reach theoretical saturation—the point at which all new data fits into existing categories. This method assured that I collected enough data to gain a thorough understanding of the questions I sought to answer. CCM also allowed for constant reflection on the study's culminating three themes presented later in Chapter 5.

Trustworthiness
Ensuring trustworthiness in qualitative research is a holistic process incorporating all stages of research—construction of research questions, data collection, data interpretation, and presentation of findings (Harrison, MacGibbon, & Morton, 2001). It is the process through which researchers meet the criteria of validity, credibility, and believability that will be assessed by peer researchers, study participants, and the reader. Researchers must provide ample evidence that their findings and conclusions are sound (Rolfe, 2006). In this section, I briefly discuss how trustworthiness differs from reliability and validity in quantitative research. I then discuss three primary means by which I established trustworthiness: (a) prolonged engagement in the field, (b) triangulation, and (c) member checks.

Trustworthiness in qualitative research is similar to reliability and validity in quantitative research, though their meanings are quite nuanced and should be used with care and purpose. According to Golafshani (2003), the primary goal of quantitative research is to construct valid, standardized instruments that ensure replicability or repeatability of results across multiple administrations. Reliability ensures the replicability of results through a high degree of stability in the instrument. Validity determines whether the research has truly measured what it was intended to measure and directly relates to the accuracy of the developed instrument.

Unlike quantitative research, qualitative research does not have as its end goal a reliable and valid standardized instrument. Instead, qualitative research is a situated activity that locates the researcher in the world with a set of interpretive, material practices that make the world visible (Denzin & Lincoln, 2000). Qualitative research yields a set of representations that makes the world better. According to Lincoln and Guba (1985), establishing the trustworthiness of research is at the crux of issues conventionally discussed as validity and reliability in quantitative research. They also discuss how researchers have traditionally posed four factors—truth value, applicability, consistency, and neutrality—in order to ensure trustworthiness within the conventional positivist paradigm. Trustworthiness is always negotiable and open-ended, and does not require the reader to accept the account without further questions or concerns. For this study, I engaged in three primary activities—prolonged engagement, triangulation, and member checks—in order to establish trustworthiness.

Prolonged engagement
Prolonged engagement requires that a researcher spend ample time with research subjects, materials, and contexts to collect enough data to reproduce a thorough and convincing portrait of the issue under study. Lincoln and Guba (1985) suggest that prolonged engagement requires that the researcher "be involved with a site sufficiently long to detect and take account of distortions that might creep into the data" (p. 302). The period of prolonged engagement is also meant to help the researcher build trust with the respondents, check for misinformation, and clear up any misunderstandings about data meaning and interpretation (Glesne & Peshkin, 1992; Lincoln & Guba, 1985).

I spent the entire 2009–2010 academic year researching Metro U. students in person. I was on campus on a weekly basis throughout the 10-month period. In addition to the time I spent with students at the Metro U. campus, I spent time visiting with students off campus in their neighborhoods. I visited their homes and they sometimes visited me at my office at the University of Southern California. During the winter and spring academic breaks, I attended scheduled IMAGINE events. I also regularly reviewed available Metro U. participants' Facebook posts and IMAGINE discussion board items. This prolonged

period of time increased the likelihood that inaccuracies during the
initial data collection were identified and addressed as the project
continued. I was able to address issues or questions with students on a
regular and informal basis during our regular interactions ensuring data
veracity.

Triangulation

Trustworthiness can also be established by triangulation—the process
of employing multiple methods, sources, and researchers (Glesne &
Peshkin, 1992; Lincoln & Guba, 1985; Merriam, 1988). Mathison
(1988) explains that in order for a study to withstand the critique of
colleagues and peers, multiple methods and data sources need to be
executed within a research study. Triangulation reduces the possibility
of chance associations, as well as systematic biases prevailing due to
repeatedly using the same method, data source, or investigator in an
inquiry (Onwuegbuzie & Leech, 2007). Further, triangulation provides
more opportunities for the researcher to gather an adequate
representation of the underlying phenomenon being researched
(Newman & Benz, 1998). As I will elaborate in the next chapter, for
example, Alejandra, a Metro U. junior, mentioned that she was
involved in several community grassroots organizations. This casual
reference was later confirmed when she repeatedly advertised various
organizations' events and fundraisers on her Facebook page and the
IMAGINE discussion board. The type of analysis I undertook to
triangulate the data provided me with greater certainty that what I have
written is factual and relevant.

   This study satisfied the demands of methodological triangulation
by means of collecting data via observations, individual interviews, and
document analysis. Utilizing multiple methods allowed me to collect
data in a variety of ways as well as corroborate my research findings.
That is, when I collected data through formal and informal observations
and interviews and the data all pointed to the same conclusion, I could
be confident in the accuracy of my results.

   Triangulation was also particularly important in the context of this
study since researching undocumented immigrants has its own distinct
confidentiality issues and concerns due to their illegal immigration
status within the US. For example, I was not able to observe the
majority of Metro U. students at their places of employment since
doing so would have required permission from their supervisors. Some

of the employers were not aware of the students' immigration statuses. However, I overcame this limitation by observing Metro U. students participating in IMAGINE meetings and other activities where I could blend in as a graduate student. I substantiated these observational findings with information collected during individual interviews and document analysis.

Member checks

Finally, I engaged in member checks or informant feedback that involved sharing information with study respondents. Lincoln and Guba (1985) believe that member checks can be a "critical technique for establishing credibility" (p. 314). Member checking is intended to allow study participants the opportunity to correct errors or challenge incorrect interpretations on the part of the researcher. Maxwell (1996) also argues that member checking is the single most effective method by which to eliminate misrepresentation and misinterpretation of the "voice" of the research. Over the course of the research project, I sought feedback from select study group participants about the credibility of the data collection, analysis, and conclusions. I focused on participants checking the veracity of the data and not my interpretations of the data. I sent drafts of Chapter 4 to a few of the Metro U. participants for review. I received feedback and minor changes from a couple of the students but most did not request any changes.

Checking in with my participants for their impressions and opinions about collected data helped me present participants' genuine experiences as undocumented college students. As I point out in Chapter 4, pursuing a college education caused tension in some students' relationships with their parents. By member checking, I provided students with the opportunity to review the often-conflicting information they shared about their relationships with their families. For instance, Manny, a Metro U. sophomore, confirmed that while his family was a traditional Mexican family that stuck together during life's challenges, he simultaneously resented his parents. This resentment intensified as he pursued a college education and began to critically question his parents' decision to have a large family with limited financial means. Checking collected data with study participants helped ensure that I accurately represented these types of data. I was able to check that students' personal accounts were accurately portrayed in the collected observations, interviews, and documents.

AN ADVOCACY/PARTICAPATORY PERSPECTIVE

Relevant to my own analysis and interpretation of the students' stories were my own beliefs and biases with regard to the population studied. I struggled to maintain a balance between my sympathetic bias toward this group of students and ensuring the integrity of the research project. My personal and professional experiences with this group of students were the impetus for my choice of study topic. I did not try to rid myself of my previous experiences and values. Rather, I accepted the role of an interpretive researcher, one that "understands that research is an interactive process shaped by [one's] personal history, biography, gender, social class, race, and ethnicity, and by those of the people in the setting" (Denzin & Lincoln, 2000, p. 6). I made a regular and concerted effort to keep separate my personal feelings from the actual data collection, analysis, and interpretation. As a researcher, I strove for a balanced perspective and presentation of data throughout this project.

My personal perspective coupled with a documented history of how educational institutions and individual experiences affect education and its social outcomes led me to approach this research from an advocacy/participatory perspective. Creswell (2007) and Reason (1994) argue that the advocacy/participatory perspective is particularly useful for the study of marginalized individuals and groups. Creswell (2007) explains "the basic tenet of this worldview is that research should contain an action agenda for reform that may change the lives of participants, the institutions in which they live and work, or even the researchers' lives" (p. 21). In this study, the issues facing undocumented students were of the utmost importance when considering students' individual paths to matriculation.

Approaching research from this perspective influenced my study in three ways. Creswell (2007) explains that one of the primary reasons for employing an advocacy/participatory perspective is to identify and expose the oppression, domination, suppression, alienation, and hegemony experienced by marginalized peoples. By exposing these sources of oppression, I was in a position to lend a voice to participants' silenced experiences. Second, advocacy/participatory research aims to raise consciousness not only about the existence of these students but also improve their realities (Reason, 1994). The knowledge and experiences of undocumented college students is thus honored and valued throughout the research process. Research participants were empowered through the process of constructing their own knowledge through self-reflection and awareness. Third, this perspective allowed me to genuinely connect and collaborate with research participants. Participants had a voice in the evolving research design and data analysis of the project.

CONCLUSION
Researching undocumented college students may have been challenging as an outsider. Gaining access and securing the trust of research participants took time and persistence. However, I felt it was important to conduct qualitative research on a group of students that is simultaneously encouraged and discouraged from participating in postsecondary education. In this study, I seek to highlight the ways in which students construct and enact their identities as college students in such an environment. I now turn to the stories of the nine Metro U. undocumented students themselves.

CHAPTER FOUR

Going to College

In this chapter, I focus on the experiences of nine undocumented Metropolitan University (Metro U.) students. Connecting the tenets of both bridging and bonding social capital to the lives of undocumented college students is best exemplified by students' ordinary experiences both inside and outside of the classroom. I provide details about these students' academic, familial, extracurricular, and social experiences. Like other undocumented college students, these nine Metro U. students do not qualify for some of the programs—namely financial aid and academic support programs—that assist first-generation and low-income students in meeting their postsecondary goals. These students navigate the college-going process without formal institutional and governmental support.

I have organized this chapter into three sections. In the first section, I provide background information regarding the 2009–2010 academic year at Metro U. The context in which these students pursued a postsecondary education is relevant given the unprecedented state budget cuts. Next, I describe each of the nine Metro U. students (see Table 5). I focus on their individual backgrounds including their living situation, socioeconomic standing, and immigration status. I also provide a brief sketch of their academic, familial, and social experiences. In the third section, I describe three scenarios involving the Metro U. students so as to provide additional context of the Metro U. campus. I now turn to a discussion of the 2009–2010 academic year at Metro U.

Table 5. Profiled Metropolitan University Student Characteristic

Name	Age	Sex	Age of Arrival	Transfer	Level	Major
Cristina	20	F	3 mos.	Yes	Junior	Spanish
Monica	22	F	11	Yes	Junior	Sociology
Julia	18	F	13	No	Frosh	Undecided
Stephanie	20	F	2	Yes	Junior	Political Science
Alba	18	F	7	Yes	Frosh	Undecided
Luz	20	F	13	No	Junior	Sociology
Alejandra	20	F	8 mos.	No	Junior	Social work
Jackie	23	F	3	Yes	Senior	Political Science
Manny	19	M	6	No	Soph.	Computer Science

THE 2009–2010 ACADEMIC YEAR

As described in Chapter 3, Metro U. was a desirable location to collect data for myriad reasons—it is a public comprehensive Hispanic-Serving Institution (HSI) located in California, home to the nation's largest undocumented immigrant population. The university also had relatively low in-state academic fees—approximately $4,900 for the 2009–2010 academic year. All of the nine Metro U. study participants qualified for in-state fees via California Assembly Bill 540 (AB 540). The 2009–2010 academic year was significantly affected by California's unprecedented budget situation. Metro U. faced a reduction of $29.5 million in state funding. Thus, Metro U. implemented measures in order to remain operational. The campus reduced its operating budget with mandatory furloughs. The faculty and staff received a 10% reduction in salary. Further, Metro U. increased student fees by 27% for the 2009–2010 academic year.

All of the Metro U. study participants were keenly aware of how the state budget cuts were affecting their postsecondary education goals. In particular, students felt the economic impact of increased academic fees. Some students could not afford the higher fees and did not enroll in one or more terms during the academic year. A handful reluctantly paid the more expensive per-unit part-time fee just to stay enrolled or graduate that year. Students were also impacted by the reduced course offerings on campuses. Starting fall 2009, course offerings were cut a minimum of 7% in each department. Students regularly complained that they could not enroll in courses that satisfied degree or major requirements. They also complained about being unable to enroll in their first-choice courses. One student arrived on the first day of spring classes to find all three of her major classes cancelled.

Besides the effects on student fees and course offerings, study participants also expressed how the budget situation impacted other facets of their education. For those students who were able to enroll in courses during the year, many had to work more hours to pay the rising costs of their education. As a result, they had less time to devote to extracurricular activities and less time to spend on campus. Metro U. students experienced reductions in their respective campus library operating hours, leaving them less time to utilize library resources and dedicated study spaces. Mandatory staff furloughs left students unable to access student services like admissions and enrollment at scheduled times during the week. Faculty furloughs forced instructors to decrease the number of course meetings during the term. Instructors also reduced their office hours as well as the time they devoted to answering students' electronic correspondence. Some teaching assistants and instructors explained to students that they could not provide comprehensive remarks and feedback on assignments due to the furloughs.

The entire campus community—students, staff, and faculty—were overwhelmingly dissatisfied with the budget situation. Education scholars and commentators questioned the feasibility of the 1960 California Master Plan's promise of free tuition with fees for auxiliary costs like dormitories and recreational facilities (Heller, 2009; Stripling, 2009). Students, staff, and faculty participated in campus demonstrations and walkouts throughout the year. Campus, university-wide, and statewide coalitions also led demonstrations protesting the budget cuts and increases in student fees at local state office buildings in Los Angeles, Sacramento, and San Francisco. Many UC, CSU, and Metro U. undocumented students joined these coalitions to protest the budget cutbacks directed at public education.

In summary, the 2009–2010 academic year was an extraordinary time to be a student at Metro U. All students were aware of exactly how the budget affected campus course offerings, class size, instructional time, programming, and campus facility maintenance. Undocumented matriculants disproportionately felt the effects of the budget cuts, as they could not access the traditional financial programs designed to assist low-income students meet the rising costs of attending college. For instance, they did not receive increased federal, state, or institutional financial aid monies to counter the increased academic fees. As a result of paying their fees towards the end of the preceding term if not early in the current term, they were also usually some of the last students to enroll in already limited courses. These realities made pursuing a college education even more challenging. In sum, a number of undocumented students took leaves of absence during the 2009–2010 academic year; most focused on saving money for when they returned to campus. I now turn to a discussion of the students themselves. I start with the nine students I spent the year with at Metro U.

NINE METRO U. STUDENTS
Christina
A petite yet athletic woman, Cristina appeared to be a young high school student instead of a college junior about to turn 21 at the end of the school year. She usually wore trendy, form-fitting clothes with her long dark brown wavy hair pulled back in a ponytail. Cristina had a serious, quiet demeanor. During our first interview, she joked that she would make a great soldier. "I am sort of serious … people think that I am mad all of the time … [or] too serious for my age." She assured me that she was not angry and did like to socialize. Cristina also took great pleasure in getting good grades as well as maintaining her karate skills. She had recently started a new relationship with an Army reservist. "I think we are starting to get serious."

<u>Family life</u>
Cristina lived with her younger brother, her older sister, and her parents in a suburban neighborhood about 13 miles distance from the Metro U. campus. "We live in a two-bedroom apartment. It's small. The three of us live in one room and my parents live in the other room. It's very difficult since I don't talk to my sister." Cristina had a close relationship with her brother. "He was born here [and is] a citizen …. He's in high school. I have helped him prepare for college …. He's the one who wants to go to military school. He can do it. Maybe like West

Point." Cristina shared an affinity for the military with her younger brother as she had planned to join the Army before she learned of her immigration status. Her older sister attended a local community college and planned to transfer to a four-year institution. Cristina explained, "The thing is my sister and I don't really get along. We don't talk at all ... never really have conversations with each other. We keep to ourselves."

Cristina's parents were both born in Mexico. Cristina's father completed college and worked as a primary and secondary teacher before moving to the United States. Her father had always planned to move to the US since he frequently accompanied his own father on business trips north. Since moving to the US 20 years ago, he had held several professional jobs, most recently working as a biochemist manager at an automotive company. He was able to have a professional job because he had a work permit and a driver's license. Cristina's mother completed middle school in Mexico and was a homemaker. She had recently started cleaning homes to earn some extra money to help pay for her daughters' postsecondary education. Cristina and her parents had a "normal" relationship. "We talk but they don't know everything about me." Cristina thought that her parents were peculiar in that her mother and father often interacted with the three children separately. "My parents tell us things separately, never together. It's sort of ridiculous ... but that's how it works with us."

Socioeconomic standing

Cristina's family's socioeconomic standing was both beneficial and problematic for the 20-year-old. Cristina was the only Metro U. study participant whose parents paid for her entire education out of pocket. She did not work, receiving money from her parents as needed. Her father received regular payments from family members back in Mexico, proceeds from an inherited business and two rental properties. Cristina's family was doing well economically. "I know that we are doing better than a lot of other people." She also pointed out that where she lived was different than where Metro U. was located. "The feedback I get from people—they say that it's a pretty good neighborhood. Now that I have seen other areas, it's a pretty decent area. It's very low on crime." Cristina was aware that the primary and secondary schools she attended in her neighborhood were better than most of the schools her Metro U. peers had attended. "I know that the schools are better where I live …. I was better prepared for college." While Cristina expressed relief that she grew up in a more affluent neighborhood and attended higher-performing schools, she also frequently discussed how she felt out of place growing up there.

> I have lived there my whole life [and I noticed that] it's different [around Metro U.] …. There was always discrimination because I was Hispanic when I was a kid. It was tough where I grew up. There were not that many Hispanics. It was [all] Armenian or Asian or White …. I have always had Asian and Armenian friends.

Cristina explained that Latinos lived in her community but the majority resided on the other side of town where housing was more affordable. The Latinos that did attend her schools never accepted her.

> I remember that the Hispanic students didn't want me around them because they always questioned why I spoke English to them. I always said that my Spanish is not that great. I can't speak to [them] the way [they] can. I just can't. I didn't know how kids my age spoke. I didn't know like … the … you know … how people speak. I just didn't know what they were saying. I was used to speaking to my parents and my family. You speak a certain way around adults … with respect. I spoke Spanish with my mom and I spoke English with my father. The kids spoke another way. It made it difficult because there were not a lot of them. There were not a lot of Hispanics when I was growing up. There was like one group. If that group of Hispanic students didn't like me, they were the only ones there. It was very hard for me to find people like me.

Cristina would have been more accepted by these co-ethnics if she had lived in a different area of her suburb and spoke better colloquial Spanish. She made a concerted effort to befriend Latinos attending her high school. "I wanted to get to know *my people* [emphasis added] during that sophomore year … even though they always thought I was different because I was in [honors] classes and they weren't." Her friendships with these Latino students quickly ceased as their differences in academic goals became more apparent. Once in college, Cristina decided to embrace her Mexican heritage from an academic perspective. She pursued a degree in Spanish literature so as to more thoroughly learn her native language and culture. Cristina joined the Latino student club at her community college. She led the club as president during her second year. She transferred to Metro U. since it was an HSI and was located in a predominately Latino area of the city. "I am studying Spanish so it makes sense that I go to school with Spanish speakers in a Spanish-speaking neighborhood." Cristina confided that she had another reason for attending Metro U. Many of her friends, including her new boyfriend, thought that she was rich. She made a statement about her actual socioeconomic standing by attending Metro U. "I am not attending a UC [campus] or a private school. We don't have that much money …. I feel better when people understand that I am not rich."

Immigration status
Cristina immigrated to the US with her parents and older sister when she was three months old. She explained,

> I don't remember anything. I don't know how I came or anything. My parents have never told me the story because they have always tried to protect me against the emotional feelings, I guess. They never wanted me to know. I never knew that I was even undocumented until way later.

"Later" meant that she did not discover that she was undocumented until 11th grade. Cristina planned to enlist in the Army after high school. "I wanted to enlist because I had a friend who … enlisted and she told me about it. I was just interested. They seemed to be paying for her college. She was traveling. I wanted to travel." When Cristina asked her mother for her social security number, her mother told her that she was undocumented.

> I went home and [told my] mom that I need this information …. "Where's my SSN?" She was like, "Oh you can't do that." I asked why. She was like, "You weren't born here." All of my childhood, I was told that I was born here. I always

believed that until then …. I was shocked. I had friends who spoke of it throughout high school. You know, I felt bad for them because they had stories. They were undocumented. I always felt for them …. Eventually [when] I figured [my immigration status] out … it hit home.

Cristina was confused by this "new identity" she received at age 16. She did not have a pending immigration case to change her status. Cristina also was confused when she discovered that her parents informed her sister a couple of years earlier. "My sister knew before I did. My mom spoke to her separately before she talked to me. Like they never had this conversation with us all together." Cristina immediately knew that she would not be eligible for financial aid. Soon she discovered that she was not eligible for a driver's license.

Cristina did not start dwelling on her undocumented identity until she started college.

I don't identify as an undocumented immigrant. I mean, recently, I look at things differently. In the last six months, there's so much that I have wanted to do so I look at things now in a different way. Before when I knew, I was okay with it besides the military. There wasn't much that I wanted to do or couldn't do.

She started to understand the impact her immigration status would have on her adult life—namely employment, social, and travel restrictions. She worried about not being able to go to bars or nightclubs once she turned 21 years old. "I will have to show my Mexican passport or *matricula* and I don't want to have to explain it to people." Cristina feared that her friends and new boyfriend would reject her because of her immigration status and its restrictions. She had avoided such embarrassing incidents in the past by blaming her strict parents for not allowing her to frequent clubs or travel out of the immediate area. She had hid her immigration status by maintaining a juvenile existence that did not require formal identification.

Being an undocumented college student
As Cristina attended a relatively high performing suburban high school, transitioning to college was never questioned.

It was assumed in my schools that we were going to go to college. Always. At least one class, it was mentioned that we were going to college. "You are here so you can go to college." That was even in the regular classes. We had workshops every other week on college. We had a lot of colleges and universities come out to our school .... My teachers gave us extra credit to go to college fairs and to go visit colleges .... It was always assumed that we would go. The majority of us went. We were made fun of if we didn't pass a class. It wasn't cool to be the kid who failed a class or got a bad grade.

Cristina's parents expected her to attend college even though the entire family was unaware of how the postsecondary system functioned in the US. They even settled in their suburb because they believed that their children would attend better-performing schools.

My parents knew about college but they didn't know about the two-year and the four-year college and the privates. I didn't really know either. I was never informed from my parents. I always had to find out on my own. They always said that I was going to college afterwards and that they can pay for it. I always had that idea. I had that idea since ninth grade—my parents expect me to go to college. They want me to go. They never said where ... they never said I had to go to Harvard. They assumed that going to any college was good enough.

Since Cristina did not know the details about applying to college, her only choice was to enroll in a community college. She enrolled in community college after high school graduation. Neither Cristina nor her sister knew that they qualified for reduced in-state academic fees via AB 540 until Cristina's second year of college; her parents paid the higher out-of-state fees for two years until her older sister found out about AB 540.

I found out about AB 540 my second year in community college. I paid out-of-state fees the first year .... I was never asked about AB 540. I left the SSN blank but the AB 540 thing was never mentioned me. Eventually my sister found out. She told my mother and then she told me. [My sister] didn't tell me about it …. When my mom told me, I went to a counselor and told them that I think that I may be an AB 540 student. They gave me a form. I read and was like, yeah, this is me. I signed it and I started to pay in-state fees. Now, the in-state fees are $26 a unit. I think the out-of-state fees are almost $200 a unit.

Once Cristina discovered that she would receive in-state fees at all California public institutions, she planned to transfer to a four-year institution. The next year, she transferred to Metro U.

Cristina woke up around 6:30 a.m. on most days. She did not have a driver's license so she relied on public transportation or rides provided by her father and friends. On school days, her commute ranged from one to two hours and involved two buses. She attended classes Monday through Thursday, usually staying on campus from early morning to late afternoon or early evening. Cristina discovered the campus undocumented student club a few weeks into the fall term. For the first half of the school year, she attended weekly meetings. She also attended a few fundraisers and political action training sessions during that time. However, as her relationship with her boyfriend progressed, she spent less time attending club-related activities.

Life outside of school
Cristina did not have any significant familial obligations as her younger brother was a teenager and her mother maintained the apartment. Her parents' only expectation was that she attend college on a full-time basis and graduate in four or five years. She taught karate classes on Friday afternoons in exchange for her own dojo membership fees. As the year progressed, she increased the amount of time she spent with her boyfriend and his friends and family.

Monica
Monica considered herself a devotee of electronic music—she embodied the dramatic, alternative music in all aspects of her appearance. The 22-year-old sociology major mostly wore black clothing with a solitary touch of color in a vest, scarf, or other accessory. Monica's dark brown hair always contained a pink, purple, blue, or green chunky highlight that framed her perfectly applied

makeup. She chuckled one day when describing her routine. "This look took a long time to perfect. I do everything myself—the makeup, the hair, all of it." Monica was shy but admitted that she was much more outgoing among her friends. She was also well read and perceptive, regularly drawing from her extensive knowledge of classical and contemporary sociological theory when discussing current events. Monica was a "Latina … a Mexican … and a Marxist" and a vocal opponent of the campus budget cuts and immigration reform. She was an eloquent English speaker, periodically breaking her impassioned speech to verify her English diction with a friend or classmate. Monica was single, occasionally insinuating that she was bisexual.

Family life

Monica lived with her mother in a small rented mobile home 30 miles east of the Metro U. campus. Her father lived in the same neighborhood, periodically moving out of the region or the state for employment opportunities. Monica was the only child. She and her mother had been consistently living on their own since 2006. However, her parents had ended their relationship about five years earlier. "My parents separated when I was in middle school. They always had a rocky relationship so I think it is better for all of us for them being separated. My parents were married for 13 years when they separated."

Before Monica and her mom moved to the mobile home, Monica usually shared a single bedroom with one or both of her parents within a multi-bedroom apartment or house. Her parents continued to live together for years out of financial necessity despite their separation. Monica explained that it was common for recent immigrants to live in this type of arrangement. "I knew other families who did the same thing to get by." Monica appreciated that amidst her parents' breakup, they chose to reside in the same neighborhood. "The stability of going to the same schools and living in the same area allowed me to concentrate on school throughout the years." Her parents also stayed in the same area since relatives settled nearby. This familial support was essential in she and her parents securing housing and employment over the years.

Monica's relationships with her mother and father were different and separate from each other. She credited living in such close quarters and being the only child as fostering a very close relationship with her mother. "The relationship my mom and me have is very out—I mean, it's open." She admired her mother for working hard and providing a better life for her in the US. However, Monica most respected her mother for choosing to separate from her father even though it was financially and culturally difficult to do so. "My mother can be old-fashioned but our relationship is built on respect …. I trust that she always has my best interests in mind." Her mother was instrumental in her pursuing a college education.

> My mom always told me that I had to get an education because she doesn't want me to go through the same things that she had to go through. She doesn't want me to have to struggle with a marriage that I am not happy with. She wanted me to have options. She has always had high expectations. She would tell me to go to college. She has always told me that I have to go.

Without her mother's support and encouragement, Monica would not have set such high goals for herself.

Monica's relationship with her father was strained. "We don't have that kind of relationship so I don't know much about him." She did not see her father often and rarely communicated with him. Monica suggested that her lack of a relationship with her father was the result of her parents' contentious relationship. Further, he was not always present in Monica's life having moved to the US before she and her mother arrived. "I respect him but I don't really have a relationship with him." Her father was unclear with what he expected from his daughter.

> My dad has never really been clear about what he expected from me and my education. He would always be very focused on me doing very well. He never told me that he wanted me to go to college and be an educated woman.

Rather he encouraged her to be a good student because he equated it with being a "disciplined child."

Socioeconomic standing
Monica's family's socioeconomic standing was "working poor or lower-middle class." Her parents each completed a few years of primary school. "I think [my dad] went up to fifth or sixth grade. My

mom finished second grade. As soon as she knew how to write, [her parents] took her out of school. She had to help with her family." While Monica's family had been poor back in Mexico, they were doing much better economically in the US.

[My] neighborhood is predominately Hispanic … [and] I think [it] is working class. There are people who are facing difficulties economically speaking. But, um, it's working class, you know. When I first got there, it was single men working. But now I see more family-oriented neighborhoods. It's not … there's not a high rate of crime or anything. It's pretty safe.

Improving their standard of living was due to both of her parents consistently working.

[My dad has] always worked. When I got here [from Mexico], he was working as an ice cream man. Then he started working in warehouses and things. My mom, ever since we got here, she works as a housekeeper and nanny. She has always worked, too. She takes care of kids at other peoples' homes.

Even with her family's improved socioeconomic standing, Monica was aware of the fragility of their success. The recent economic recession impacted her parents' ability to work.

Things have gotten more comfortable over time. Except now with the economic crisis, we are kind of struggling …. [My dad] is unemployed right now …. [My mom has] lost … well, she used to babysit for two different people. She lost two of her kids and she lost her weekend job, too. Now, she is only working during the week.

Monica was constantly concerned about money throughout the academic year. Her mother and father usually gave her extra money for her school expenses. As her parents' wages decreased, her parents ceased their economic support. "I have always paid for school on my own. But, the money they gave me sometimes helped me buy gas for the car or a train pass or a book—things like that."

Immigration status

Monica immigrated to the US when she was 11 years old. She traveled
with her mother since her father was already working in the US. "He
had already been here for six years. So, we just came to meet him
….We went [to where we live now] and I have been living there since
we got here." Since Monica was 11 years old when she left Mexico
City, she was aware of her mother's plans to move to California.

> It was all of the sudden … rapidly … I didn't even notice. You
> know one day I was over there and the next day I was here.
> We came here in the trunk of a car. We paid someone to come
> here. People like have connections and the person was a
> complete stranger, completely detached from us. My mom and
> I traveled together. We were here the whole time. We crossed
> in Tijuana. I mean, we just got there on a plane and the next
> thing you know we probably spent like half a night and the
> next morning we were here.

Unlike Cristina, Monica always knew that she was undocumented.
She had witnessed her working-class parents navigate life in the US
without drivers' licenses and work permits. She adapted over the years
as she secured multiple jobs and internships while in high school and
college. Monica explained that it was because she had to "put herself
out there in the open … as a productive adult living [her] life" that she
eventually accepted and embraced being undocumented.

> I came [to college] and I was like, "I am not going to tell
> anyone about my status. I was like, what's the point?" When I
> started to get involved [on campus and in the community] and
> see all of these kids get involved with these other non-profits
> and being activists, it empowered me to be less afraid to say,
> "I am here, I am undocumented, I am Latina." I identify as an
> undocumented student, an undocumented immigrant, an
> undocumented woman, a Mexican …. I think that I went from
> having this stigma of being undocumented to now using the
> label as empowering. I think being excluded from things
> because of my immigration … excluded from things that I
> want to do kind of made me be a more dedicated individual in
> everything I do. I have had to be stronger and more outspoken.

I have had to like defend myself and just take these stereotypes and not believe them. I don't want to believe them. I don't want to be them. As an undocumented student, if I had not been undocumented, I probably would have been a completely different person. I would have been more apathetic towards education and social problems and stuff. Being part of a minority, I know how it is like to struggle in a system that is not created for you.

She reasoned that because she had no means by which to change her immigration status under existing laws, she had to continue pursuing her goals.

As far as I am concerned, there is no way that we can qualify for anything. The vast majority of my family that are here are undocumented. I would hope to change my status. As far as I am concerned, if immigration reform doesn't pass, then, my only other option would be marriage but that would sort of be cheating the system. But that's not an option for me.

Being an undocumented college student
Pursuing an undergraduate degree had been a lifelong goal for Monica. "Living in poverty in Mexico, you know that education is the only way out. You always envision going to the university." She explained that she was at the top of her elementary school class in Mexico and always held herself to high academic standards. Once she immigrated to the US, her desire to attend college shifted. "I wanted to prove that just because I am undocumented doesn't mean that I can't perform just as well as everyone else." Monica enrolled in the local elementary school in the beginning of sixth grade with no English language skills. As a high school student, she enrolled in mainstream English-only classes. During the last three years of high school, Monica took all Advanced Placement (AP) and honors classes. "I think that [I learned English] mostly because I was pushed to grasp it as quickly as possible."

Monica also enrolled in the Advancement Via Individual Determination (AVID) Program. In AVID, Monica learned about attending college including eligibility requirements, application procedures, financial aid, and matriculation. "I was in this program for four years. There's a lot of talk about college. [Not going to college] wasn't really an option in that program .... You were supposed to go to college." Unlike Cristina, Monica was well informed about her postsecondary options. AVID presented Monica with the opportunity to work closely with her AVID instructor and take classes with the same students over a four-year period.

Monica took advantage of the resources held by this close-knit group of AVID students, instructors, and counselors. During 10th grade, she indirectly disclosed her immigration status to her AVID instructor. "My teacher gave me this form and the form asked me about an SSN. I didn't put anything. He asked me if I had one. I told him 'no.' He was like 'okay' and then that was that." From that point on, her AVID instructor provided her with information about undocumented financial resources like AB 540 and scholarships. "He also helped me make practical decisions about where to go." He helped her make a comprehensive financial budget for college. Monica eventually told a few of her close friends that she was undocumented and discovered that some of them shared the same status. "We asked each other what we were going to do and stuff like that .... I mean, I knew other undocumented people in the school but they weren't really focusing on going to college .... It helped." Monica gained admission to several UC campuses, including UC Berkeley, and a couple of private liberal arts colleges. She decided to enroll at a local community college due to her financial circumstances.

Monica's mother's former employer helped her enroll at the community college where he was employed. He helped her secure a Board of Governors Waiver (BOGW) that paid her enrollment fees. As a BOGW recipient, she was also able to access the Extended Opportunity Program & Services (EOPS) resources at her college. "All of this helped me get through community college." She worked to pay for the rest of her community college expenses and saved as much money as she could towards transferring to a four-year institution. She enrolled at Metro U. because it was the most practical and affordable.

> I use AB 540 for the lower fees .... Sometimes I do drive to school if I have to stay really late even though I don't have a [driver's] license .... Most days I take the train to school. I come to campus three or four days a week.

Monica was completing her second year at Metro U. She planned on graduating in 2011. "I had to take the term off last fall because I didn't have enough money to pay .... I have enough money for [this year]. But, I am not sure about next academic year." Her uncertainty about how she was going to finance college affected her ability to commit to participating in the campus undocumented support group. "I have a leadership role this year but next year I don't think that I can spend as much time on campus. I have to work more." She was also involved in the student protests against the budget cuts and increased fees. Monica knew that if the academic fees continued to increase, she would not finish her bachelor's degree in 2011. Nevertheless, she was confident that she would complete her degree and move on to graduate studies.

> Ideally I would like to get my Ph.D. in sociology .... Maybe political science? I have thought of getting a master's degree after this but I have not started planning until now. I think I haven't planned because I cannot really grasp it economically—like how I would do it .... I hope it happens.

Life outside of school

Monica's life outside of school was typical of a young adult. She worked at a nonprofit organization on intensive five-week community-based empowerment and education programs. She used the earnings to maintain her car, pay for school, and help out with household expenses. When she was not working, she usually stayed close to home. "My mom is afraid when I go to raves or concerts or even bars since she thinks there'll be raids .... [or] a cop will ask me for my driver's license." Monica also spent time with her friends and extended family members. She made it a priority to spend time with her mother when the two were home. "I do a lot for not *really being here* [emphasis added]."

Julia

Julia was a demure 18-year-old freshman at Metro U. She was petite with long straight black hair that contrasted her pale skin. She wore makeup every day that included a rosy pink lipstick. Even though Julia was soft-spoken, she smiled frequently. "I like to look happy and ... I always blush a lot when I smile," she explained. She had not yet selected a major and was slowly adjusting to college life. "I am thinking maybe of business ... maybe something else, but *not English* [emphasis added]!" Julia neither thought that she spoke English well nor did she think that she would ever really do so. "I have a thick Mexican accent. I can't do anything about it .... I am still very Mexican." Julia acknowledged that she was a good student. "I usually get good grades. That's because I try harder than most students who are [native-English speakers] .... I want to always get good grades."

Family life
Julia resided with her parents, eldest brother, and younger sister in a two-bedroom apartment 16 miles distance from Metro U. She was the fourth child out of five total; she had two older brothers aged 30 and 26 respectively and two sisters aged 22 and nine respectively. Her second-oldest brother had been deported and lived in Mexico. Julia's older sister lived with her new husband in Hawaii. The family apartment was less crowded and somewhat more conducive to her life as a college student since her siblings' departure. She shared a bedroom with her younger sister while her parents occupied the other bedroom. Her brother stayed in the living room.

> It can get crazy .... I get work done in my bedroom that I share with my little sister. She does her work in the room and then she goes outside and watches TV. I can study that way. If my little sister is bugging me, [my parents] tell her to stop bothering me.

Julia came from a "mixed status" family. "My big brother is a citizen, my parents are [U.S.] residents, and my brother in Mexico and my sisters and I are all Mexican citizens." Both Julia and her eldest brother, a U.S. Army veteran, were the first in their family to attend college. "He's trying to go to community college with his G.I. Bill and I am going to [Metro U.]." Julia had a close relationship with her parents and her siblings. "We usually get along because there are so many of us I think. There's always someone around to talk to or hang out with." She was particularly close with her mother, often sharing her plans with her mom and asking her for advice. "She and I talk a lot .... She is very proud of me because I am going to college. She always wants to know what I am doing."

Julia had a healthy relationship with her family since they all had specific responsibilities within the family unit. "It's better in [my family] because we all help out." Her parents both worked full-time jobs—her mother worked at a factory and her father worked as an air conditioner technician. Julia's eldest brother also contributed economically to the household with earnings from his part-time job. Julia's primary responsibility was supervising her younger sister. "It's my responsibility to get her ready for school and get her there on time. I check her homework, too."

Socioeconomic standing

Julia's socioeconomic standing was typical for the community where she resided. Like Monica, she lived in a predominately Latino neighborhood. "We are Mexicans … working class …. Most people around here are like us." Her parents both finished primary school back in Mexico before they went to work to help care for their families. They expected their children to achieve a higher level of education. "My parents expected me [and my siblings] to get more education than them. We had to at least finish high school. My mom always said that we had to go to school." Her parents sent their eldest son to live with relatives in California when he started high school. He was the first person in her family to graduate from high school.

> [My eldest brother] changed things for us—well at least for all of us except my other brother in Mexico; he only finished eighth grade. [My parents] saw that [my eldest brother] could finish [high school] and that helped me and my sister to finish.

Julia's older sister completed secondary school in Mexico while Julia completed high school in the US. Her younger sister was on track to graduate from high school. Julia enrolled in college immediately after high school while her brother postponed community college matriculation until after he completed his military service.

> It was different for me than him …. He came here by himself and then went to the military to get job training and help my family out. He's the first born son so that was expected from him …. I was lucky because I could just go to college after

high school and not have to give my parents a lot of money for rent and bills.

Julia's family lived paycheck to paycheck with modest savings for use in case of emergencies. "Even though my parents are [U.S.] residents, we live modestly." Her family's economic situation was better than many undocumented students' since her parents and eldest brother could legally work and possessed drivers' licenses. Her parents had still struggled to find consistent work over the years. "Like everyone, we have struggled since arriving here …. My parents have little education so they have not always been able to find work …. My mom works in a factory and sometimes she doesn't work for a few weeks." This situation had worsened over the years when her parents lost her siblings' economic contributions. "When my brother was on active duty, he didn't always have money to give us …. My other brother was deported …. My sister used to help us but now she is married. … [so] we have struggled." Julia started working as a restaurant cashier in high school to help out her parents with money. "My parents don't charge me rent or anything. They don't ask for help but I will give them some money sometimes."

Immigration status
Julia immigrated with her parents and siblings to the US in 2005 when she was 13 years old. Since Julia's family was mixed status, their journey to the US was staged.

> My parents came here in the 1970s and then they went back to Mexico [after my eldest brother was born]. When [my eldest brother] was 15, he came by himself to the US [and] lived with my uncle and aunt and that was it. Right after high school, he went to the Army. He petitioned for my parents so they came here with green cards …. When [my parents] got here, me and my sisters stayed with my mom's friend back in Mexico. My parents were here for two months and then [my mom] went back to get us …. At the time, I didn't get what was going on. I was just like kind of lost. My mom talked to a man. After two days, the coyotes went to pick us up and me and my sisters came in different cars with a guy. My mom just drove across with her green card. My little sister and I drove

across in a car. Then they went back and got my older sister. When we were about to pass the borderline, I was kind of lost. They gave us a name and told us to memorize it. When we crossed, we waited for a day and then drove north.

Julia and her family settled in their current neighborhood six months after they arrived.

Identifying as an undocumented immigrant had always been part of Julia's life since arriving in the US. "I have always known about my status …. My family is mostly undocumented—us, my cousins—it's not a big deal in my family or my neighborhood." She did not believe that she had ever been discriminated against because of her status. "Maybe that's because I don't share it with most people?" Julia did not dwell on her status. "I think about it when I am going to fill out some applications or when I am going to apply for a job. When something is formal, I think about it." She had recently felt more uncomfortable and out of place as she became more aware of her surroundings.

I do sometimes feel different than everyone else. There are some places that you will feel awkward. Like when you go to a public event. I feel different. Let's say, uh, like when there is a presentation. Sometimes I feel different in my classes. Like right now I have a liberal studies class. We are talking about Latinos. I feel like they talk about it but they don't really know how it feels like to be undocumented and come here. They are talking about immigration. They just talk about immigration. Maybe most of them don't know about us? Maybe their parents are immigrants and they are not? I feel like a lot of them are talking about it from their parents' perspective.

These difficult moments were occurring more frequently as she transitioned to adulthood. "I think that even if I knew about what was going to happen to me here in this country, I would have still come to the US [if my parents had not brought me]."

Unlike Cristina and Monica, Julia did have a pending immigration application (see Table 6). Her parents filed an immigration application for Julia and her younger sister about five years before. "I don't know the details but they said that they filed. I hope that I get it soon … before I graduate." She did not worry much about securing a professional job without documentation. "I think that I am going to finish [my degree] in about five years …. I have time to figure things out." Julia hoped that the DREAM Act or comprehensive immigration reform would pass during that time, shortening her wait for residency.

Table 6. Students' Immigration Details

Name	Pending Immigration Application	Mixed Status Family
Cristina	No	Yes
Monica	No	No
Julia	Yes	Yes
Stephanie	No	Yes
Alba	No	No
Luz	No	No
Alejandra	No	Yes
Jackie	Yes	Yes
Manny	No	Yes

Being an undocumented college student
While Julia's parents always had high aspirations for her educational attainment, she did not seriously consider attending college until she started high school. In Mexico, she had considered college impractical due to the cost in lost wages and tuition.

I think the conditions that we lived in when we were in Mexico also pushed me to [think about going] to college here …. My parents always talked about us coming here so that we could get better jobs and an education …. I was interested in going to school even then.

Julia was overwhelmed with learning English when she started eighth grade in the US. She enrolled in English as a Second Language (ESL) courses at both her middle and high schools. Because she focused on learning English, other subjects were not a priority. "I could have done better … may have been admitted to better colleges but I just focused on English." Julia spent three years in ESL courses before moving to English-only courses. As Julia became more confident in English, her goal of attending college became more realistic.

Julia's high school also helped her prepare for college. Her high school not only prepared every student for college admission, it also provided specialized assistance to undocumented students. "I went to a high school named after the man who helped start the AB 540 law in California .... Everyone at the school was really focused on going to college and helping undocumented students." Staff and instructors encouraged all students to attend college, regardless of their immigration status.

> The school started talking about college when I was in 10th grade. That's when they started talking about the high school graduation exam .... After that, they started talking about college and careers. I started to get interested in it .... When I started to get interested in college, the counselor would arrange appointments with each of us and then talk to us. She was my regular counselor. I started to meet with her. She asked me where I was planning on going to college and how I was preparing for it. She told me which classes to take .... I learned about the differences between the CSU and the UC and the community colleges in 11th grade. The principal and the teachers and the counselors were really focused on us going to college. I would use the computers at school to look at information.

Julia discovered early in high school the challenges she would face as an undocumented college student. "Another AVID teacher would help us, too. I found out about AB 540 in 10th grade. The AVID teacher told us about the affidavit and all of that stuff .... I knew I couldn't get financial aid, too."

Julia benefitted from the school's focus on preparing all students, including those who were undocumented, for the rigors of college. Julia, along with many of the other undocumented students at her school, felt comfortable sharing their status. She and her friends founded an undocumented student support group.

> I was in a group for AB 540 students. We created one at our high school. We were the first generation from that school .... Me and my friend knew other people who were in the same situation .... In the beginning there were no more than 10 of us

[in the group]. In 11th grade, there were more people coming to the meetings ... allies and AB 540 students. Then there were like 15 students. We would meet every Thursday after school. We would talk about our situations and where we wanted to go to school. We were all looking to go to college. That's what we talked about ... how are we going to [go to college]. We talked about what we needed to do and who we needed to talk to and stuff. I was one of the leaders. My volleyball coach who was also my history teacher would let us meet in his classroom.

Her high school group consulted with a local UC campus undocumented student support group for advice and support. She participated in the group until she graduated in 2009.

Julia's high school experience was instrumental in preparing her to transition to college. She was both knowledgeable about college preparation and matriculation.

When I was in 10th grade, I created a plan about how I was going to go to college. I was like I am going to take these classes during the summer, I am going to start working, and I am going to keep working around the year to get money to go to college. I started to work during that summer. I have been a cashier in a restaurant since summer 2007. I graduated high school in 2009. During the school year, I worked on the weekends for 16 hours. I saved all of the money. When I started college [this year] ... well, I got a $1,000 undocumented student scholarship from the parents' booster club at my high school .... I had another $2,000 that I had saved .... I applied to [public four-year] schools that were close to me since I don't drive and take the bus .... I knew from the beginning that I had money for over half of my first year. So, I decided to go to Metro U. instead of [a community college].

Julia's college plan was comprehensive; she planned on only having to take one or two terms off during her entire undergraduate career. She was a one of a few students from her high school that enrolled at a four-year institution as a freshman.

Since starting Metro U., Julia joined the campus undocumented student support group. She hoped to benefit from the college group as much as she did from the high school group. "[The group] talks about the classes I should take. I talked to the [Educational Opportunity Program] EOP counselor who helps us even though I am not in EOP. I already had problems getting classes so she's helped me with that." She planned to take advantage of their other resources—scholarships, employment opportunities, school supplies, and volunteer opportunities. Julia helped with outreach efforts involving undocumented high school and community college students. She felt that earning good grades and attending graduate school would encourage fellow undocumented immigrants to attend college.

Life outside of school

Julia's first year of college challenged her non-academic life. She started the academic year working two jobs—her weekend cashiering job and an afterschool job as a coaching assistant with her school's volleyball team. She quickly learned that she had over extended herself.

> I got really sick in the fall. I was working too much during the week. I couldn't do it with the long bus ride because I am on the bus three hours a day …. My mom was worried and she told me that I had to quit.

Julia quit the afterschool job at the end of the season before the winter holidays. "I just work the weekend job and go to school now … [and] it's a lot better for me." Julia also spent a considerable amount of time socializing with her family. "We have parties and stuff together all the time."

Stephanie

An attractive young woman, Stephanie appeared more mature than 20 years old. On some days she arrived to school looking particularly fashionable, combining formal business wear with trendy accessories. On other days, she presented herself in typical college student fashion wearing jeans and a T-shirt. "I am running for student council so sometimes I have to look more formal than other times." Stephanie transferred to Metro U. at the beginning of the year. She was bright and well spoken, standing out among most of her peers in class and social settings. She often engaged people with casual conversation and took the lead in classroom or group activities. "I like to participate in things—whether it's in class or on campus …. I don't want to be one of those people who just sit by while others do things and I watch." Stephanie had become more politically aware of the plight of women and immigrants during the course of her college studies.

> These things are important to me …. First I think that I consider myself as a woman and then second I think of myself as undocumented …. It's personal …. That's why I am a political science major—I want to know more about why things are the way they are.

Family life
Stephanie lived with her parents and 17-year-old brother in an apartment eight miles distance from Metro U. Similar to Cristina, Monica, and Julia, Stephanie had lived in the same area since immigrating to the US with her mother and father. The family changed residences throughout her childhood depending on their financial situation.

> We have lived in many different places. We lived with some distant relatives that offered us a room for a while …. We have lived with my dad's friends [and] we stayed in a garage for a while. When I was in elementary school, we started living in apartments on our own.

Stephanie's family life was "normal." All four family members got along well and supported each other. She spoke with pride about her younger brother who was finishing high school. "He was born [in the US] so he can get financial aid. He's a good student. He'll go to a UC." She mentored him, helping him prepare for college since he started high school. Stephanie also had a close relationship with her parents. "They have done a lot for me and I am very grateful." She respected her father for his accomplishments despite growing up in poverty. "My grandpa was absent most of the time because he was an alcoholic. So, um, my dad along with his older brother had to sustain the entire family." She admired her mother for being goal-driven and persistent. "My mom has been really involved in my life and education …. I respect her a lot because she had aspirations to have a real career. She has always put us first and works hard to accomplish my family's goals."

There had been recent tension between Stephanie and her parents. She credited the tension to her growing up and spending more time away from the family. "My parents are traditional Mexicans …. I am their daughter and my father thinks that when he says something, I am going to listen and that's it." Her mother and father were displeased with her extracurricular schedule that left her less time to help out with the family's flower shop. They were also upset that she was considering moving in with a friend. "They found my birth control pills so … they think I want to move out so I can have sex all of the time …. They aren't happy about me dating either." Stephanie hoped that she and her parents could resolve their differences. "I think a lot of it has to do with me going to college …. I have guilt over it …. I know that I am a different person than them because of my experiences. I just see things differently."

Socioeconomic standing
Stephanie classified her family as "working poor …. I would say that I grew up in very low-income neighborhoods." Similar to Monica and Julia, Stephanie lived in a Latino neighborhood. "It's homogenized … everyone is Latino and there are no other cultures." Both of her parents finished high school in Mexico. Her father studied engineering for one year before he dropped out to support his family. Stephanie's mother was a professional secretary in Mexico. As her parents struggled to make ends meet in Mexico, their resettlement to the US became more apparent. "[My dad] had worked in the US doing construction before he married my mom and after I was born. He was aware of the opportunities in the US …. My parents decided to move permanently for a better life."

Stephanie's father supported the family on his construction worker salary for many years. "He got a little bit above minimum wage but my mom didn't have to go to work at the time. So, given that we couldn't really have a large apartment, it wasn't difficult to live on my dad's income alone." Stephanie had a better idea of her family's financial situation as she grew older. "[We] didn't really have luxuries but we still had everything that we needed. Maybe not as fast as others got things … like beds or computers and stuff. We got them eventually."

The family's needs eventually exceeded what her father alone could provide.

> When I started going to high school, my dad was kind … well, we were kind of pressured for my mom to get a job because my dad after a while could no longer work construction because he was like … it was physical deterioration. He has a lot of back problems and stuff like that. So, he stopped.

Her mother found work at a fast food restaurant and her father supplemented his existing part-time music career with a full-time job at a movie theater screen factory. Her mother's additional income afforded the family a more comfortable life. Stephanie's mother eventually left her job as a fast food restaurant manager to open up her own flower shop. Unfortunately the shop was not doing as well as the family had planned. "The flower shop we currently have is not creating enough profit for us to live off of. So everything that we make is reinvested in the flower shop." This situation had recently put more pressure on Stephanie's family to make ends meet. "Nothing has been easy for my family but I think that things will work out."

Immigration status
Stephanie, like Monica and Julia, had always known about her immigration status. "I am not sure why I knew, I just knew about it." Stephanie's immigration status was comparable to Cristina's—her younger sibling being a U.S. citizen would not aid her own immigration status in the near future.

> I would like to change my immigration status soon. But, currently the laws are established and I have no way of even considering filing. I don't have any relatives here. My entire family is in Mexico. No one can claim us. My brother will be able to claim my parents and me [in a few years] but that's even a difficult process. So, at this point, there's really no way for me to file to change my status.

While she did not have means to change her status, Stephanie and her family had been able to secure U.S. visas when she was younger. "My father got a work permit as a musician. So, with that visa and permit we were able to travel to Mexico and visit my relatives and come back without a problem … We visited twice." Those visas had since expired. Stephanie and her parents' undocumented status had affected the family over the years. "I saw my parents limited to working particular types of jobs …. I have been limited to the jobs I could get, too." Stephanie's employment history included food service worker at her mother's old fast food restaurant, sales clerk at a large retailer, and data entry clerk at a nationwide gym chain. "Actually, my parents purchased papers. I was able to present that as my identification [when applying for jobs]." She compared herself to her U.S.-born brother. "He can get a driver's license and I can't. He can also get a job anywhere and get financial aid for college …. I can't do these things legally even though I work and I drive."

Stephanie's public existence led most people to believe that she was a documented immigrant, if not a U.S. citizen. However, she was aware that she belonged to a distinct underclass. According to Stephanie, most Americans thought that undocumented immigrants were menacing and undesirable.

> I think that they treat us pretty badly. I think that there are a lot of stereotypes related to how people treat undocumented immigrants …. Instead of seeing the immigrant population as something that is good for our country, we are just looked down upon as a burden on social programs and stuff like that.

Stephanie challenged these negative assumptions with research and her personal story.

> I personally try to do research on studies that say the opposite. That way if I am confronted by a person who says these things, I have evidence to back up that immigrants do pay taxes … like the ITIN that we use to file. I have been filing every year …. I talk really openly with other students about the fact that I am undocumented. I do it because in a way people who don't come from that background can see that and see that there's nothing that I am really doing that people can say that I am being a burden on the system. If anything, I am being a contributor due to the fact that I work and go to school. Some people just have this perception that we are just

here to live off of the system and that we plague cities with high crime rates and stuff like that. The reason why I tell people is so that they have a perception of a day in a life of a person who is undocumented. I think trying to make that emotional connection with people is a way that we can kind of combat those stereotypes. I think that this status does just alter your world perception .... It has made me kind of sensible about how I treat people and how I treat members of my community.

Stephanie's academic and career goals were challenged as she transitioned to adult life. "I think I am like everyone else who is in this position—I don't want to stress out about it but I cannot help but think that I am going to be held back because of my status."

Being an undocumented student
Stephanie had always been a good student. Her parents stressed the importance of education early on. "My parents always emphasized that an education was really important." Her mother took primary responsibility for Stephanie's educational training. "[My mom] actually taught me to read and write in Spanish before school. I learned my multiplication tables when I was three or four years old." Her teachers took a particular interest in her development and education. School administrators and teachers were more receptive to her parents' requests than those of other parents because of her academic abilities.

[The teachers] recognized that I was really an excellent student. At the time that I enrolled in school, they had that distinction between Spanish- and English-speaking classes. I was in the Spanish-speaking classes. I didn't know a word in English .... My mom demanded that they change me to English-speaking classes [so I could learn] .... They took her seriously and changed me to English classes.

Stephanie transferred to an English-only class in first grade and was fluent by the end of the year. "I don't say this with any arrogance or anything but I surpassed all of my classmates like in everything that had to do with writing, reading, and everything. I was a really good student."

Stephanie's parents' involvement in her education continued throughout the years. When faced with having to transfer to another school one year, her parents offered to find a way to stay at the school.

> I think that there was something about that school that I felt a sense of belonging and [my parents] sensed it. Since I had been there for so long, there wasn't anywhere else where I wanted to be but there. Even though the school was underfunded, you could tell that the teachers really cared and the fact that we had such small classes, we can make those connections with teachers that could really help us.

Because the school was a K–12 learning center, Stephanie remained at the school until she graduated high school in 2007. Classes were small, with a graduating class of approximately 150 students. She excelled academically, consistently placing on her school's honor roll and enrolling in all of the available honors and AP classes. Stephanie also thrived in her extracurricular activities. "All throughout high school, I was really involved in clubs. I didn't do sports but I was part of the science club, the academic decathlon …. I was school president …. I did a lot of things like that." Her learning center also provided a safer school environment. "It was a great school for being an inner-city school. I think that the main concern was the high pregnancy and dropout rates, not gangs or drugs."

While her primary and secondary school experiences were largely complete and rewarding, her preparation for being an undocumented college student was incomplete and dissatisfying. Her high school experience was similar to Cristina's high school experience. "My parents expected me to go to college but they didn't know how that was going to be and how I was going to be able to go to college … I relied on people at school to help me figure out a plan." She did not receive adequate information about how to prepare to go to college as an undocumented student.

> There was no orientation at my school about how to go to college in this situation. We had a college counselor but he never really made an attempt to research outside … I guess he just relied on what he already knew. The only thing that he recommended was for me to apply strictly to private schools.

They would be able to give me funding so that's what he told me. In regards to the resources that I was getting through school, there was really no college fairs that the school provided ... like scholarships and stuff.

Following her counselor's advice, Stephanie only applied to private schools. She was admitted to two highly selective liberal arts colleges but could not afford to attend. Stephanie became despondent during the end of her senior year, believing that she would never be able to attend college. "I didn't know about AB 540. I didn't know I could go to community college and then transfer. I was this great student yet I didn't know anything about going to college." At the end of her senior year, her college counselor finally told her about AB 540. She enrolled at a local community college and transferred to Metro U. two years later.

Stephanie mostly credited her parents with helping her pursue a college education (see Table 7). They insisted that there was a way for her to attend college and pledged their support.

So, then, my parents [were] just like ... "we understand that you want to go to college but you need to kind of help us out. You are going to go to school but you are also going to get a job." That's when I started community college. I got a job, too. I actually got two jobs before I started going to community college.

Stephanie paid for all of her school expenses with her own earnings from the data entry job. She developed close relationships with some of her community college instructors.

My professors were able to guide me and provide emotional support that I didn't really find elsewhere. At my school at the time, there wasn't an AB 540 support group ... And so, I was kind of disoriented. After a while, I was kind of like I have to stop with this negativism. I had to try to be optimistic and be involved. I got involved in stuff. Since then, college life seemed to lighten up and I actually looked forward to going to school. I have kept my GPA really high. Then when I transferred here to Metro U., I feel even more motivated because I feel that I was able to make that transition even more successfully.

Stephanie was elected as both a college student representative to the campus-wide student council and as the president of the campus undocumented student group in May 2010. "It's going to be busy my senior year but I will manage. I want to do a lot of outreach to the undocumented students on campus." Stephanie planned to graduate in spring 2011.

Table 7. Students' Key Supporters

Name	Parents	Older Sibling	Friend(s)/Partner
Cristina	X		
Monica	X		
Julia	X	X	X
Stephanie	X		
Alba	X	X	
Luz	X		
Alejandra	X		
Jackie	X	X	X
Manny	X		X

Life outside of school

Stephanie spent most of her time outside of school working. She worked between 25 and 40 hours per week. Once she transferred to Metro U., she worked more hours to pay the higher academic fees. She scheduled her work hours in the early mornings and late evenings depending on her class and public transportation schedules. Stephanie also spent time with her family either at the flower shop or at home. "I usually end up working at the flower shop or hanging out at home with them." Stephanie started dating a fellow Metro U. student at the beginning of the 2009–2010 academic year. "We are the same major so we can study a lot. He's a little older than me. We get along so I am happy."

Alba

A sporty and petite young woman, Alba was a youthful looking 18-year-old freshman at Metro U. She dressed like a typical teenager—

usually pairing jeans and a T-shirt with her high school cheerleading warm-up jacket. Alba always wore her medium-length dark brown hair down or in a haphazard ponytail. She sometimes roamed campus in her workout clothes. "I am taking softball this year so sometimes it's easier to come [to school] with my workout clothes on …. I run late sometimes." Alba was attentive to others while maintaining a reserved demeanor. She became particularly animated when she interacted with her close friends. Alba had a deep, raspy voice that in many ways was uncharacteristic of her physical appearance. "People have asked me if I smoke because my voice is … what do you call it—deep—no, no, no—raspy. Yeah, it's raspy … so, I try to speak loudly so people can hear me."

Family life
Alba resided with her father and older sister in a small single apartment in the heart of the city, approximately 10 miles distance from Metro U. "I have lived in the same place I live now … well, only with my father since I was 12 years old. I just live with him. Well, now my sister lives with me, too." Her sister—age 23—recently moved back to her father's apartment after she broke up with her boyfriend. Alba's father—age 67—welcomed his eldest child back home. "He's old now and he can use the extra help and money from my sister." Alba's mother lived a couple of blocks away in her own apartment. Her parents separated when she was 12 years old. Alba consistently resided with her father. She never considered living with her mother even though she had maintained a close relationship with her over the years. "My father wanted me to live with him when they split …. I was able to help him out since he's old …. We get along."

Alba's family was close-knit even if their time together was limited. Alba's parents maintained a relationship over the years. They cooperated with each other in the best interest of their daughters. Her parents shared a single common goal—improving their daughters' opportunities and quality of life.

> My mom and dad still have a relationship. They talk because of me and my sister. My mother is with another person. My mom is younger than my dad so I guess it never really worked out. She's 43 and he's 67. I am the only daughter between my mom and my dad …. My mom met my dad when she was

pregnant with my sister …. He has always treated my sister as his own child …. They want what is best for us … a good education and a better life than we had in Mexico.

Alba regularly confided in her mom about issues relating to school. "I tell my mom about school because even though she doesn't understand a lot of it, she knows that I worked hard to get [to Metro U]." She shared some of the details about her daily life with her father, too. "I usually cook dinner for him so we have some time to talk about our days then." Alba's relationship with her sister was the least developed. "We are just different from each other …. She left the apartment a while ago and now she is back. She works nights so I don't see her a lot." Alba and her sister did occasionally talk about personal issues. "My sister sometimes talks to me about her life …. But I don't talk to her about [Metro U.] since she didn't go to college and I don't want to make her feel weird about it."

<u>Socioeconomic standing</u>
Similar to most of the students profiled in this study, Alba's family was working class. Alba compared how she and her family lived in Mexico to how they have lived in the US. The main difference was the diminished sense of safety and security where they lived in the US.

We have [always] lived in working-class neighborhoods. Back [in Mexico], we lived in the south where it is really poor. But, we were never afraid of violence. Where we have lived for the last 10 years [in the US] … it's busy and hectic. There are a lot of gangs. Starting from when I was in middle school, there were always shootings and fights. Me and my friends and sister never played outside. We stayed inside because it was safer.

Alba adjusted to the new environment when she moved to the US. She and her family were still better off living in an urban environment in the US rather than in a poor, rural area of Mexico. "I just have to think about what I do and where I go here. That's really it."

Alba, as with Monica and Stephanie, was more aware of her family's economic situation as she grew older. "I used to think that we were doing okay but as I get older, I see how close we are to being really poor again." Her entire family had always been poor. Her immediate and extended family members received minimal if no formal education in Mexico and the US.

> My mom lived in a little town in Oaxaca so she only went to second grade but she was really old—like 16 years old—when she finished second grade. She knows how to write and read. My dad went to middle school … maybe like seventh grade. My entire family has either no education or no higher than my father. The majority know at least how to write …. My sister stopped after 10th grade in the US.

Despite their low levels of education, Alba's parents and older sister consistently secured employment, albeit low-wage jobs. "Back in Mexico, my parents were always struggling to find jobs …. At least here they have found work more easily." Alba's family survived on low-wage employment because they all pooled their money together. Her mother had worked as a cook in two different restaurants—one Greek and the other Mexican/Salvadoran. Her father briefly worked at two different carwashes before securing a job at the Greek restaurant. Alba's sister started working full-time jobs—first as a babysitter and then as a seamstress—when she was 16 years old. Her sister recently worked as a server and hostess at a cross-town restaurant. "[My sister] works the night shift so the money is better."

Her parents and sister had constantly dealt with the imminent threat of losing their jobs. Similar to Monica, no one in her family had legal permission to work. "None of us have work permits or drivers' licenses. [My parents and my sister] know that they could get let go at any time." Alba's mother and father, similar to Stephanie's father, suffered from physical ailments over the years that affected their ability to work. "Working has been tough for [my father] because of his age …. He's worked hard all of his life and his body is tired." Thus, it had been challenging for her father to continue to work in labor-intensive jobs. Her mother injured her leg while working in the restaurant. "She started getting bigger and bigger … I guess [the injury] affected her. It wasn't her weight but her leg started getting bigger. We never knew what happened because we could not go to the doctor or anything." Her family's socioeconomic status had been affected by limited access to health care. "We have never had insurance …. When we get sick or get hurt, we don't go to work or school …. [My parents and sister] don't get paid if they don't go to work."

Immigration status
Alba immigrated to the US with her parents and sister when she was seven years old. At the time, her sister was age 12 and mother and father were age 33 and 56 respectively. Her family's move to the US was the last of many and frequent relocations.

> When we left, I was in second grade …. [My family] came [to the US] all at one time …. When I was smaller, we would always travel everywhere for work. I was never at a stable school. I was always from one school to another school. The job … they used to sell cheese …. We would have to go and get it. We lived in Oaxaca and then Mexico City and then we moved again. We would always move. They would tell us that we would be moving here or there …. I don't have an exact number of how many times we moved but I remember moving in kindergarten twice and then in elementary school, we moved four or five times …. We moved a lot. It was all because of economic reasons …. The reason we came here was because we always had an economic struggle.

Her family's economic situation was dire by the time her parents made the decision to move; her parents' cheese business did not sustain the family and her father's age thwarted his attempts at securing work. Further, her parents feared that their daughters would have to leave school soon to help support the family. "My mom's brother was already in [California]. He told her like … that she could work [there]. They told my parents that they could get jobs here … so we flew to Tijuana … [and then] we crossed on foot."

Alba's experiences in the US had been positive. She considered herself a Mexican American. "I have intentions of going to Mexico to visit but I don't want to live there. I feel like I have adapted [to the US]." The only issue that remained unresolved was their immigration status. "We are all undocumented. Nothing is going to change for us without [immigration] reform." Similar to Julia, Alba's immigration status had affected her life but she did not worry about it as much as other people.

I guess I think about my status more as I get older... [At Metro U.] there is a point where you feel like you are the only one in a classroom in this situation. But, I just don't think about it that much .... I know that I am not the only one.

Alba's opinion of her immigration status was based on her beliefs that she had a better life in the US even as an undocumented immigrant. Her status, while not ideal, still afforded her a higher education.

I think undocumented immigrants are treated pretty well. I mean, we have opportunities here. We come here to have a better life. I mean of course they try to exclude you ... like you cannot work legally. But at the same time, it's not that bad. They still let you work with a fake social. They let these things happen. Of course if they wanted to stop it, they would just stop hiring people. I could tell you that they treat us really bad because of the way I emotionally feel about it. In the same way, they help me get scholarships and I can still go to school. These are the things that matter to me. If I can finish college, I can find [a way] to make the other stuff work.

Being an undocumented college student
Alba started third grade at the local elementary school. She remembered being sad the first few years she lived in the US.

I remember this period of time that I felt really discouraged .... I didn't know that I was going to come here and not know anyone or the language. I didn't really understand how different it would be here.

She enrolled in ESL classes where she remained for four years. "I was in ESL for third and fourth grades. Then I stated fifth grade in English-only classes. I learned the language pretty quickly. I had ESL [again] in sixth and seventh grades." She struggled with formal English as evidenced by her return to ESL classes in middle school. She credited her return to ESL classes on being bused to a middle school in a more affluent part of the city. "They had higher standards in [the other school]."

Alba became very interested in going to college while attending the other middle school.

> I started thinking about going to college when I was in middle school. People would talk about going to high school. There were some people who would talk about going on to college. Everybody would be like I want to go to college. Through time, I always liked school a lot. I always wanted to go further. I figured I would go to school until someone told me to stop.

She discussed her interest in attending college with her mother and father. They did not fully understand her goals but were generally supportive of her plans. "They never told me 'no' even though they didn't understand what I wanted to do .... My parents would try not to discourage me."

Alba was placed in a Special Learning Community (SLC) for the first two years of high school. She qualified for her high school's new magnet program because of her high academic performance. She was still unaware of how her high school record factored into her college plans.

> I started escalating to the higher classes in ninth grade. That year, I got really good grades because I just liked school. There was a period of time that I didn't know that high school would determine the type of college I could go to. I didn't know that it would specifically determine my options. I started doing really good. I just started escalating more.

Alba credited her transferring to the magnet program and participating in a local mentoring program for her successful preparation for college. "I didn't know much. I slowly started learning about these things that would help me go to college."

Once Alba began receiving professional college advice from her mentor and magnet counselor, she was able to plan for college (see Table 8).

> My [mentor] didn't really know about AB 540 in the beginning. But, I told her about it. Then she found out more

about it and helped me. I also told my friends who were AB 540 in high school. Whenever someone said that I or they couldn't go to school, I would want to yell at them. I felt that if they said that I couldn't go to school and it threatened me. I would get really worried. It has always been a worry for me. I knew that my parents would not be able to pay for anything. I knew that for a fact.

Table 8: Key Institutional Agents

Name	H.S. Teacher	H.S. Staff	College Instructor	College Staff	Mentoring Staff
Cristina					
Monica	X			X	
Julia	X	X			
Stephanie		X	X		
Alba		X			X
Luz		X			
Alejandra	X	X			
Jackie	X			X	
Manny	X			X	

Alba, similar to Monica and Julia, worked with her mentor on creating a comprehensive college plan. She applied to several UC and CSU campuses as well as private institutions that offered scholarships to undocumented students. She also attended local financial aid seminars presented by the state's student aid commission. At the seminars she met Metro U. undocumented students who eventually helped her acclimate to her new university. "When I found out they had a support group at [Metro U.], I wanted to go there. I knew it would help me." Alba enrolled at Metro U. as a freshman in fall 2009 as an undecided major.

Alba's first-year college experience had been positive. She placed into remedial English and math courses. "I knew I was behind the other students but I feel better now that I am taking the [remedial] courses." She participated in the campus undocumented student support group. Alba attended local and statewide immigration reform retreats and rallies. She made a few close friends at Metro U., too. The only concern

Alba had about her college education was how she was going graduate in a timely manner.

> My parents can't help me because they have no money. I had about $6,000 in scholarships to start school but that isn't going to pay for the whole first year with the bus and books and stuff. Some of the scholarships will give me money for another year or two. I am looking for a job but it's bad right now …. I don't want to take a lot of terms off because I don't want to get that behind and lose hope.

Alba also struggled with how to include her family in her education.

> I guess you could say that they are innocent … they don't know anything … I wish they understood what I am doing and how it will help them one day. I know they believe in me … [but] it would be good if they really understood.

Life outside of school

Alba's non-academic life revolved around her parents and her friends. She was responsible for taking care of her father—namely cooking meals and cleaning the apartment. "I know he works hard. He's so tired when he gets home from work so I try to help him by cooking and cleaning. I go out after I finish taking care of him." Alba also spent time visiting her mother when she was not working. She found time to hang out with her four best friends from high school. She and her friends made more elaborate plans when their other friend came home from school in Boston. "When she comes home, we all see each other and go out …. She has been supportive of me going to college. We are proud of each other." Finally, Alba devoted some of her time to finding a job. "It's important for me to find a job. I don't want to give up on college. I need money fast."

Luz

Luz often entered a room carrying a container of food. The 20-year-old Metro U. junior seemed to always be running late, never able to finish a meal. "I eat and eat and never gain weight! I try to eat all of the time." Luz was thin and petite with long wavy brown hair with bangs that grazed the top of her eyes. She usually wore jeans and a sweatshirt to campus. Luz always carried an over-sized backpack that seemed to swallow her back whole. "*Everything* [emphasis added] is in this backpack!" On the weekends, Luz went salsa dancing with her friends and boyfriend. "I love to go dancing." Luz was inquisitive, never shy to ask for help or advice. She majored in sociology and hoped to attend graduate school in the future.

Family life
Luz lived in a one-bedroom apartment with her mother and younger sister 10 miles from the Metro U. campus. Her father resided in Mexico even though her parents were still married. "He comes and visits us once or twice a year. He prefers living there … and he still has his business." Luz's family had a nontraditional living arrangement mostly due to her younger sister's medical treatment. Before her second birthday, Luz's sister was severely burned in an accident. Unsatisfied with the treatment her sister received in Mexico, Luz's mother found a hospital in California that agreed to treat her daughter free of charge. Luz's mother and sister started traveling to the US a couple of times a year in 1996. They would stay for three months at a time so as to accommodate a surgery or other treatment. Luz remained in Mexico with her father during these medical trips. In 2002, Luz's parents decided that it would be best to for Luz, her mother, and her sister to live year-round in the US. They told Luz that this plan was the only option given their family's medical, educational, and emotional needs. At age 13, Luz, her mother, and her sister moved permanently to the US.

Luz was very close to her parents and sister. Much of her relationship with them revolved around accomplishing their family goals.

> I love them so much. I admire [my parents'] courage for making the decision to get my sister the medical care she needs. It has been hard being separated. Being undocumented and doing the medical treatments has not been easy for anyone. When my father comes, we celebrate and enjoy our time together.

Luz had significant responsibilities within the family. Similar to Julia, Luz was expected to set an example for her younger sister and help her parents manage the family's affairs. Luz's responsibilities fostered a particularly close relationship between she and her sister.

> My father isn't here and I speak English better than [my mom]. My mom depends on me to do a lot with my sister .... I go to her parent-teacher meetings, I am responsible for her after school, I help her with her homework. I am sort of like her other parent because my dad can't be here to help and my mom is busy with work. Plus, she has needed extra help because of her health issues .... I have been there to take care of her and make sure she is doing what the doctors tell her to do .... I am her big sister, her friend, her nurse. We are very close.

Luz drew motivation and inspiration from her family in pursuing her own goals. "They help me a lot by just being [themselves]."

Socioeconomic standing

Luz's family was "between working class and working poor .... We seem to be always working and saving money. We try to save, but then something comes up ... the car, bills. I don't drive. But always something happens." Her parents had an elementary school education; her mother completed sixth grade and her father completed fourth grade. Before Luz's mother relocated to the US, she owned and operated a *taquería*—a small taco shop that sold prepared food items. Her mother mainly found work as a nanny and housekeeper in the US. Luz's father owned a small market in their hometown in Mexico. Her parents did not share money with each other. "My mom's money goes to living here [in the US]. That's it .... My dad supports himself in Mexico." Luz regularly gave her mother money for rent and paid for the family's cell phone bill. "It's not a lot—like $200. But, I know it helps my mom out."

Over the years, Luz's family had adjusted their living situation and standards to what her mother could afford. Her mother and sister originally lived in a van to save money. This arrangement no longer was feasible when Luz arrived. Her sister's hospital found the family temporary housing with a family of four that lived nearby. "So, we were seven living in a one bedroom apartment. My mom had to look for [another] place ... because we just slept there. You can't live with strangers like that for long." Later her mother found a garage to share with another family. "This was better because we were only sharing the kitchen and the bathroom." The garage was not ideal given her sister's proclivity to infections and illnesses. Her mother then secured an affordable single apartment. Recently the family moved to a one-bedroom apartment. "It makes it easy when my father visits. There's more room. Plus, my sister and I need more space to do our school work."

Luz's mother chose to live in their current neighborhood because she felt that it was safer and offered more opportunities to her family.

> I live near a big private university so it's not that bad. It's working class and mostly Mexicans and other Latinos but then there are the people who live in the area who work at [the university] or go there. It's quiet in my neighborhood and the police are around so it's a good place to live.

Her neighborhood benefitted from the various university neighborhood programs and the presence of middle- and upper-class students, staff, and faculty. "It's better than where a lot of people live." Luz benefitted from living close to the university as she frequently studied in the library. She also enjoyed interacting with the university students.

> I knew that I couldn't go there ... it's too expensive .... But, when I would shop across the street at the market, I saw the differences between those students and the [neighborhood] residents. I wanted to have what they have ... a college education and a better life.

Immigration status

Luz's immigration status was different than the other Metro U. student participants. She and her family had all received non-immigrant tourist visas because of her sister's U.S.-based medical care. Using the visas, Luz and her family were able to visit the US for limited periods of time; the visas did not allow the family to stay extended periods of time or immigrate to the US. Luz, her mother, and her sister were undocumented immigrants since they had violated the terms of their tourist visas. As was the case with Stephanie's visa, Luz's and her sister's visas had expired. Luz's mother's tourist visa was still valid.

Her mother feared being separated from her daughters and never traveled outside of the country. Luz's father had never violated the terms of his tourist visa. Thus, he freely traveled back and forth from Mexico to the US to visit his family.

The family's immigration situation affected Luz's identity as an undocumented immigrant. Since her father could still visit the US, the impact of her parents' choices was not fully realized. "We have not been isolated from my family or anything. We know what goes on in Mexico …. It's important that my father can visit us because we know that we are going to be able to see him." Luz's immigration status was different than other undocumented immigrants because of her sister's medical needs.

> My sister came here to see the doctors since she was a baby. She started to spend so much time here that she was getting used to it. Her medical treatment has been going on for 13 or 14 years. It's going to take a lot more surgeries and procedures. It doesn't make sense that if she stays here for long times that her family can't be with her.

Luz considered being separated from her mother and sister as unnatural. "We had no other choice but to come [to the US] and stay. Me and my sister need our mom."

Luz determined that her presence in the US was a human rights issue, not an immigration issue. "I have a human right to remain with my family as my sister gets medical treatment. I don't control how long her treatment is going to be." She did not focus on being an undocumented immigrant. Rather, Luz explained that her status had positively contributed to who she was as a student, daughter, and friend.

> I think that being undocumented has helped me in a way. It has made me stronger. It has made me more responsible in terms of school and working. Probably, I wouldn't be where I am right now. I always strive for the best and go the extra mile. For me, it has been a good experience.

Similar to Stephanie, Luz felt responsible for educating the American public on the realities and myths about undocumented immigrants. "I think that we have to do some work on that and educate people about the truth. I feel like we have to engage in a conversation with [the American public]. We have to give them information …. There are misconceptions."

<u>Being an undocumented college student</u>
In Mexico, Luz was a competitive student. She had wanted to go to college since she began her formal studies. "Since I was in kindergarten, I have wanted to go to college. I always liked school and I always wanted to go. If I had finished middle school and continued, I would have gotten the university scholarship they give." Like Stephanie's parents, Luz's parents demanded that she do well in school. "My parents have always had high expectations for my education …. Sometimes [my mom] would tell me not to work or do something so that I could focus on my school." Her parents continued to support her educational plans when she moved to the US. "Now they expect me to continue with it."

Luz enrolled in eighth grade in the US. She was surprised how being an ESL student affected her preparation for college.

> When I started middle school here in the US, I was taking ESL for two years. I started in high school and the counselor … as an ESL student, they put you down and they don't encourage you to do AP or honors classes or anything like that. I only took AP Spanish. I was in regular classes. Those ESL classes, they are two periods instead of one. For that reason, I was behind in algebra, science, and government …. I was always taking summer school and extra period classes, too.

Early on she identified the differences between going to college in Mexico and the US. "I had to be a lot more involved here with my education than there." She reached out to her college counselor for help during the 10th grade. "I told her that I was undocumented …. [The counselor] knew about [AB 540] so she told me …. She really cared and she was really dedicated …. I paid attention [to what she said] and that's how I learned." Luz learned about college requirements and completed the necessary courses and tests. In lieu of filing a FAFSA, her counselor encouraged Luz to attend the same local financial aid seminars Alba attended. "I found out about scholarships and that

[Metro U.] had a support group. I started attending the [support group] meetings in high school. The people there really encouraged me to go to college."

Luz's college plan was comprehensive and practical.

> I only applied to CSU [campuses]. I knew that I would not be able to get into a UC [campus] and I would not be able to afford it …. My college counselor told me to apply to campuses I knew would accept me.

She also secured $1,500 in scholarships for the first year of college. She decided to attend Metro U. since the fees were relatively low and she could commute from home. "I wanted to stay around for my sister and my mom, too. [My sister] is looking up to me for support and help with going to school. I will be done when she starts college." Luz paid the first year of college with scholarship money and her mother's savings. She enrolled in one or two community college classes concurrently to save money. After the first year of college, she paid all of her fees with her own earnings.

> I have served food … worked at a call center … and did data entry at a nonprofit. I quit a couple of months ago because I was so tired so I am looking for temporary work. I will work full-time at the nonprofit this summer to save for my last year …. I will finish. I know that now.

Luz's participation in Metro U.'s undocumented student support group was instrumental in her progress as a college student. "I have found jobs from the group …. I have got books from members … [and] rides to campus and work." She also represented the group within a statewide coalition for immigrants' rights and immigration reform. "I have traveled because of the group. It's been great." The group's membership gave her the strength to persevere.

> My fellow members … they are so smart. A lot of them … two of them got their master's degree and one of them is applying for a Ph.D. even though he has not been that involved. So, they always encourage me …. Just the fact that

they are doing it, it just proves that we can do this. The ones of us that are struggling, we know that it is possible.

The support she received from the Metro U. group enabled her to more freely share her status with other students, staff, and faculty members. "They probably don't think that undocumented students can actually go to college and get a master's degree or a BA. I tell people I am undocumented because they need to know that this is possible for people like me."

Life outside of school
Luz's life outside school revolved around her work, family, and friends. She worked either before or after school and on weekends when available. Luz had substantial responsibilities with her younger sister. "Even though my sister is in 11th grade, I still have to make sure she is doing her stuff especially since she misses school because of her surgeries." Luz spent time with her boyfriend and friends, too. "He's busy and I am busy so we may only see each other once a week." She enjoyed resting at home when she had the time. "That's a luxury I don't know much of!"

Alejandra
Alejandra was a feisty 20-year-old junior studying social work at Metro U. She was average in height with brown hair that she occasionally highlighted. She wore glasses and always wore the latest trends. "I work in the fashion industry so I just know what is going on and what people are wearing." She was a typical college student balancing hectic work, academic, and social schedules. Alejandra was also a serious community organizer. She was a self-described "revolutionary" who fought for her beliefs and rights. "Some people would say that I am [a] radical [but I say] that I am a strong and independent *mujer* .... I define myself that .... I will fight for my beliefs and the struggles of my people." Alejandra also identified as a *raza educator* who organized for increased access to *raza studies* for members of her community. As a member of *la raza*, she was regularly subjugated because of her race and background. "I am responsible for being the best I can be so my people can have a positive role model .... It's up to me."

Family life
Like Cristina, Julia, and Stephanie, Alejandra came from a mixed status family; her younger sister was a U.S.-born citizen while she and her parents were undocumented immigrants. She resided with her parents and 19-year-old sister in a rented two-bedroom house 10 miles distance from Metro U. Their house was one of two houses on a lot in an aging residential area of the city. "The place is old .... I share a room with my sister and my parents have the other room .... It's small but it works." The house also doubled as her mother's place of business—a daycare facility for a few young children. "She takes care of kids so it can get really crowded and loud." Her father was unemployed. "He usually works in construction. He's not working right now .... He tries to help out around the neighborhood and help with my mom and the kids she watches." Both of her parents completed high school in Mexico. "My father did some college classes when he was in federal prison here in the US. He never earned a college degree, though. He started with ESL classes and stuff." Her sister had recently graduated from high school.

Alejandra's relationship with her parents was "extremely close and open. We talk to each other. They help me plan my life because I respect their opinions and their experiences." Her positive relationship with her parents allowed her to be successful in both her academic and personal pursuits. "They provide me with a good example. I am just following their lead." Alejandra's relationship with her sister was less positive. She often disagreed with her sister's choices. "She is just ... well, we just are not alike. We have a lot of disagreements. I love her but she is not doing the right things with her life." The tension had increased over the past year since her sister forwent enrolling in college. "She wastes [her citizenship] and doesn't even go to college .... The only thing she will do that is good with her citizenship is sponsor my mom's immigration application." Alejandra's father was ineligible for U.S. residency since he was a convicted felon.

Socioeconomic standing
Alejandra's family, like Monica's, Stephanie's, and Luz's families, was "working poor." Her family had always struggled to keep up with living expenses. Particular periods had been more difficult than others due to her parents' varying income. Alejandra and extended family members periodically helped support her immediate family.

My father was in jail between fourth and eighth grades. I started to work at the flower shop across the street from my house during this time. My mother and uncle mostly supported us. I gave them some of the money I earned from the flower shop. I didn't mind because I was helping my family and that's what I believe in. Now since my father has lost his job in construction, it's only me and my mom working .... So, we have always usually lived paycheck to paycheck.

Alejandra gave her parents money as needed during high school and college. "I give everything I make to my mom after I pay my school expenses. I work between 18 and 27 hours a week now. In the summer, I work six days a week for about 50 to 55 hours." She hoped that her younger sister would soon help pay the family expenses. "My younger sister just got a job .... I have not been able to save much since I help my mom with the rent and some of the bills. Now my sister will pay some of that."

Alejandra's family had always resided in the same neighborhood. The area had transitioned from an African American majority to predominately Latino. "Even though the people have changed, it's still a working-class, poor neighborhood. People are working but not really getting ahead. We're struggling here in this capitalist imperialist system." Alejandra explained that her neighborhood had been neglected by American society largely because of its racial composition.

The social structure is based on race. The history of America has been written by race. Class was dictated by race. White would be superior and so forth. For me, race is everything. It goes to policies, it goes to education, it goes to any economic standards. If you look at the poor and the working class, then you see race .... America has portrayed the Black and Brown communities as negative. So, they don't want to be part of that negative aspect .... I see that in the community.

She thought she had no choice but to stay and help those with fewer opportunities. "I have to help out my people who are on this side of the border."

Immigration status

Alejandra arrived in the US when she was eight months old. She traveled with her mother and father across the border. Like all of the students profiled in this study, Alejandra's family left Mexico in search of better economic and educational opportunities in the US. "There's a reason [my family] came here ... for opportunities that were taken from us by the American government and NAFTA and all of the policies over history." Her parents settled near family already living in California. Some relatives were undocumented while others were U.S. residents and citizens. Alejandra did not have a pending immigration application. When her sister turned 21, she could petition for Alejandra. It would take anywhere from 10 to 15 years under current law for Alejandra to receive U.S. residency. "I don't even think about it as an option."

Alejandra, was unaware of her immigration status until she reached eighth grade. At that time, she received a scholarship that required her social security number and other personal information. Similar to Cristina, she asked her mother for the information.

> I didn't know the whole politics about it because I was so young. I knew that I was Mexican, put it that way. I didn't know that I was undocumented. I didn't know that you were supposed to have papers. I get the scholarship and the check is ready to be given to me and we were ready to go to the ceremony to get it. I asked my mom for my SSN. She said that I didn't have one. I thought it was like a phone number. I asked her for a phone number to put and she said that I couldn't do that. My sister is a U.S. citizen. So, my mom sort of compared us. "Your sister was born in [the US] and you were born in Mexico. So you were born in Mexico, you are not American. Because you are Mexican, you don't have an SSN." I went to the scholarship people and told them the story my mother told me .... That's when the counselor said, "Oh, you're undocumented."

Alejandra's discovery that she was undocumented immediately changed her reality; she began to question her accomplishments and her future plans.

I thought that if this money was taken away from me, what else is going to be taken away from me? I didn't know what to do with it. My mom was kind of telling me more about it. She said that I need to be careful about who I tell about it because not a lot of people like it. Inside of me, I felt different.

Discovering that she was undocumented was life changing for Alejandra. She credited her sociopolitical radicalization on discovering her immigration status. Joining community grassroots organizations focused on empowering both immigrants and non-immigrants provided solace. "I decided that I wasn't going to be oppressed anymore. I took action by getting involved in learning about *la raza* and the issues that affect us." Learning about immigration issues was influential in Alejandra deciding to attend college. She befriended immigration attorneys and learned about immigration law and policies.

When I was learning about my culture I started to figure out why I was undocumented in the land that used to belong to my people. I started to figure that out. Why am I being deprived? Why are these institutions oppressing me? …. You either give me papers or you don't give me papers. For the immigration reform, I am not looking at it as an *amnesty* [emphasis added] …. If the legislation says "amnesty" I would not apply either. I am not going to say "sorry" for being here. Amnesty is like saying, "Oh, I am sorry, I give up, here, give me papers."

Alejandra neither felt guilty about being undocumented nor did she feel that she owed anyone an explanation of why she wanted to stay. Alejandra, like Monica and Luz, viewed her immigration status with respect and dignity. "I don't let it—being an undocumented immigrant—identify me. I don't see it as a source of weakness or depression. I see it as my source of passion and inspiration."

Being an undocumented college student
Alejandra's primary and secondary educational experiences had been mostly positive. Many members of her extended family had attended school in the US. Her mother took an active role in Alejandra's education. She enrolled her daughter in a Head Start pre-kindergarten program at age three. Alejandra then transitioned to the local

elementary school where she participated in after-school and summer programs. Her mother regularly met with teachers during the school year to monitor her daughter's progress. Alejandra's mother encouraged her to learn English by practicing with English-speaking relatives and friends. She was fluent in English by the beginning of third grade and placed in the honors program in fourth grade. Alejandra attended one local middle school and two local high schools; she enrolled in all of the available honors and AP classes. "I always remember school as something fun …. I always went to the same schools. My mom knew the teachers and was involved. I always felt like I was connected to the schools and people there."

Alejandra's parents expected her to do well in school and follow the example set by a few of her family members who had attended college. They provided her with opportunities to pursue her academic interests.

> I started to think about college when I was young. It was like in middle school. My cousins … one of them actually graduated from [a private university]. One of them went to [a CSU] and then got a master's degree at [a UC]. I knew that it was middle school, high school, and then college. That's how I knew about college. My mother would always ask what I needed to do for school …. I had to get good grades. If I was sick, I had to go to school. My parents always made me go.

Alejandra researched college admission requirements and developed an academic and extracurricular plan for high school.

> I was excited about going to college and learning. I wanted to do something different than a lot of the kids I grew up with …. When I found out I was undocumented, that's why I got so upset. I saw my plans out of my reach.

Alejandra changed her college-going plans when she learned that she was undocumented.

> I knew I was going to be the experiment for being an undocumented student in my school. The first thing I did was tell my teachers and counselors about my situation. I told my

friends, too. I told anyone who would listen …. Everyone—
the teachers and counselors—were surprised that I was open
about my status and I was going to apply to college and not go
to a community college.

Sharing her immigration status with others placed her in a position to
acquire pertinent information about being an undocumented college
student early in the college preparation process. One of her teachers, a
former UC admissions counselor, told her about AB 540 and
undocumented student scholarships. Similar to Monica, Julia, Alba, and
Luz, institutional agents encouraged her to network with undocumented
high school peers and local college students to learn about their
postsecondary plans and experiences. "By the time I started 11th grade,
I had a plan. I wanted to go to a UC, I had started saving money … all
of my teachers paid for all of my applications. I was ready."

Senior year of high school was bittersweet for Alejandra. She was
valedictorian and gained admission to the most competitive UC
campuses. She also earned $8,000 in scholarships for her first year of
school. Still, she was unable to realize her dream of attending UC
Berkeley.

I sat down with my parents and we figured out where I could
go. They were able to commit to helping with books and
transportation …. I really wanted to go to UC Berkeley. But, I
couldn't. It was a far, far reach even though I got in there.

Alejandra enrolled at Metro U. because of the lower costs and vicinity
to her home. "I wasn't thrilled about it but I accepted it …. I have been
able to go through without any breaks." She continued her involvement
in grassroots community organizations. Alejandra's experiences at
Metro U. had been overwhelmingly positive. She joined the campus's
undocumented student support group and took the lead in coordinating
AB 540 presentations at local high schools. Alejandra was also
involved in Metro U.'s campus budget cuts coalition. She often found
herself as the bridge between some community organizations and
campus student groups. "People know me because I get their
scholarships and volunteer. I hook people up with each other." Being at
Metro U. provided her with the unique opportunity to make deep and
lasting connections both on campus and in her community.

Coming to [Metro U.], I have met so many professors that through sharing my story, they would offer to lend me or buy me books …. My comrades have supported me and helped me stay in college …. I even have a sponsor who will sponsor me during my senior year [at Metro U.] …. He will pay for my tuition but if I get enough scholarships to pay the fees, he will pay for an on-campus apartment …. He has sent me to Sacramento and has helped me emotionally over the years. He knows my family.

Alejandra expected to complete her degree at the end of the 2010–2011 academic year. She planned to enroll in a master's of social work program at a private university or the UC in the future. "Maybe I will be able to get financial aid by then? I will figure something out."

Life outside of school
Alejandra's extracurricular life revolved around her work responsibilities and her close friends and family. She worked year round in a wholesale fashion outlet. She also held significant duties within one community organization separate from Metro U. "We are a nonprofit so I am in the office about five to 10 hours a week. I help manage the bills and stuff." Alejandra carved out time once or twice a week to see her boyfriend. "Our families are from the same town in Mexico so I see him at family events, too …. We see each other during the weekend but I need my space away from him. He understands that I'm an *independent mujer* [emphasis added]." Midway during the school year, Alejandra's boyfriend gave her a promise ring. "We want to get married but not right now …. He's a U.S. citizen. I wouldn't be getting married to him because of that but he can help me with the residency." Alejandra spent time with her parents and close friends when she had time. "I am lucky because I have a lot of people in my life that support me and who I am. They don't try to change me and that's good because I am not changing for no one."

Jackie
Jackie was an energetic 23-year-old senior studying political science at Metro U. She was about 5' 2" with dark skin and long, layered dark brown hair. In the middle of the academic year, she dyed her hair blonde. "I used to get my hair done all of the time but that's before I

decided to transfer to Metro U. and I had to save all of that money."
Jackie usually paired her modern-looking eyeglasses with casual
clothes—jeans and a Metro U. or professional athletic team
sweatshirt—when on campus. "I like to dress up on the weekends and
for events but it takes time and costs money and I am not trying to
impress people at campus." She greeted individuals with a bright smile
even though she was often reserved with unfamiliar people. Jackie
spent most days on campus studying, attending class, and overseeing
the undocumented student club's activities and events. "I'm president
of the club this year so it takes a lot of time."

<u>Family life</u>
Jackie was the fourth of five children ranging from the ages of 15 to 32.
Like Cristina, Julia, Stephanie, Luz, and Alejandra, Jackie's family was
mixed status; Jackie, her parents, and three older siblings all were born
in Mexico while her younger sister was a U.S.-born citizen. Over the
years, the living arrangements had changed as older siblings moved in
and out of the family home. Jackie currently lived with her parents, her
two sisters, and three nieces in a rented house approximately 13 miles
from the Metro U. campus.

> We have lived in our current place for about five years. We
> live in a back house and my brother lives in the front house.
> [Our house is] really big. There are four bedrooms, two
> bathrooms, a basement, a garage, and all that. I have my own
> room, my younger sister has her own room, my parents have a
> room, and my older sister moved back in with us since she is
> getting a divorce. She has three girls. They all share the last
> room.

Jackie's house served as the primary gathering place for the family.
"My other siblings and their families come over to see my parents and
us. There are always kids around and there's always a lot going on."
    Jackie's family was "a traditional Mexican family—there's a lot of
us and my parents are in charge ... well, my dad is in charge." Her
parents both worked—her father was a landscaper and her mother was
a babysitter. The dynamics of her family changed as she and her
siblings aged.

> When I [was younger], my dad was very strict. He would
> come home from work and he would make us [kids] go run.
> We were supposed to be ready with our jogging clothes. We
> would run a few miles every day. He liked to run. We did that
> until I was in high school …. My mom, she just started
> working about three or four years ago. She was always at
> home before that. She went to work because she was bored in
> the house.

Jackie's family now revolved mostly around her younger sister, nieces,
and nephews. "I feel like I have to set an example for all of the kids.
My parents expect me to do that, too, since I didn't have kids or get
married young. My example shows them another way of life."

Jackie's relationship with her family members varied. She had a
close relationship with her parents. "We had some tough issues but now
that they see me graduating this year, I think they trust me. I think that I
have now earned my dad's respect." As with Cristina, Julia, and Luz,
Jackie also shared a close relationship with her younger sister and
nieces. She helped them with their homework and sometimes
represented her parents and sister at school activities like parent-teacher
conferences. "If I can make it and help out my sister or parents, I try to.
I want the girls to go to college and that means being involved in their
education." Jackie was not as close with her older sister and a few
extended members of her family. "As I got older, I saw their decisions
and thought that they could have done better. I guess that's just what I
think happens to family members."

Socioeconomic standing
Jackie did not label her family's socioeconomic status as "working
class" or "working poor." Her parents had a basic elementary school
education that prevented them from moving away from labor-intensive
jobs. Similar to Stephanie's father, Jackie's father supported the family
on his salary alone when the children were younger. They lived in a
garage for a year until they arranged to live in a relative's apartment.

> From the garage, my aunt owned a few units in an apartment
> building. We moved across the city. We were living with
> another person … my aunt's father-in-law. He lived in one

bedroom, my parents lived in the other bedroom, and all of us kids were out in the living room.

The apartment was overcrowded and chaotic. The family was relieved when they were able to move to a house a few years later. "We could do this because my oldest brother started working and my sister, too. [My brother] only dropped out to help my father with money." Jackie's older siblings continued to contribute to the family's expenses as they transitioned from high school to full-time work. She noted that all of the jobs her siblings pursued were in the service sector, too. "They were doing the same types of jobs—working in restaurants, taking care of kids." Jackie's eldest brother talked to her about finding a job in a restaurant when she was a junior in high school. "They didn't expect me to drop out but I had to start working. I started to work in high school. I was pretty much told that I had to work by my brother."

The family's socioeconomic standing both benefitted and suffered from more members working. Jackie and her family's living standards increased with the extra money. "Yeah, it got better. We moved to a house and my dad wasn't as stressed out. Things were more quiet .... We could get things that we couldn't get before." The drawback was that they could only afford to rent a house in a less expensive area of the city. Jackie quickly noticed that the quality of her education decreased when she transferred elementary schools.

> I guess it's when I got over to [my new elementary school] is when it was kind of like, "Oh my God!" It was really loud. The teachers didn't care. The kids were rowdy. The teachers were just there sitting, watching them. I think that they didn't have hope for the students. They figured that they were just going to be running around .... I missed the other school.

While her family was better off living in their own house, she was also disadvantaged because the neighborhood was more depressed. A friend's grandfather explained these socioeconomic differences to Jackie.

> [My friend] from the same middle school ... her grandpa used to pick us up from school .... He would talk to us the whole ride. He would explain to us ... we would go from a good

neighborhood to a bad one and he would ask us if we would notice something different. We would be like, "Oh yeah." He would explain, "Do you notice that in the good neighborhood the grass is always nice and green and in the bad neighborhood it's always dry and really high because it's not cut? He said that the people living in the areas with dry uncut grass are trying to make these other houses look beautiful in the good neighborhood. They forget about their own because they have to work harder" …. It made sense to me and I started to think about my family.

Jackie's increased awareness about socioeconomic and class issues eventually influenced her educational and career goals. "I always think even now that if we are the 'middle class' then who are the poor people? We have these things because people are working together. I knew I had to get better jobs than my family."

Immigration status
Jackie immigrated to the US when she was three years old with her siblings. Similar to Julia's family, Jackie's parents decided to stage the immigration in waves.

First my father came, then my mother, and the rest of us came a year later. I don't remember how we did it. We crossed the border with *coyotes*. I remember that I was sitting in a car with these two men. I do remember that we ran across the freeway. I was holding my mom's hand and she was holding it so hard. Maybe it was early in the morning? I think that it was here in California. I have never asked … maybe I should ask? …. They drove us to where my dad was waiting. It was my mom, me, my sister, and my brother. My oldest brother stayed in Mexico for another year and then he came to the US.

Her parents decided to immigrate primarily for economic reasons. Her father's farming no longer supported the growing family. "It was before NAFTA but it was already bad for my family. Small farmers in Mexico couldn't compete and keep working." Her father decided to try out the employment market in the US. "My uncle had come to the US before so my father used him as support …. By 1990, my whole family was here."

Like Cristina, Jackie was surprised to learn that she was undocumented in high school. "I am not sure why I was surprised. I sort of knew that my family members couldn't just go to work anywhere but I didn't understand what it was." Jackie's AVID advisor requested students' personal information at the beginning of 12th grade. Jackie asked her mother for her social security number and other immigration information. Her mother told her that she did not have a social security number.

> I told her what I needed. My mom was trying to tell me like, "No, it's not going to happen." I was like, "No, it's really easy. Once I do this, it's really quick and it's going to be online and …" I felt like I wasn't explaining it well enough. Maybe she wasn't hearing me? Maybe I didn't want to hear what she was telling me? She was like the only thing I have for you is an ITIN number. She showed it to me. She was like … "Maybe you can use it?" I was like, "No, the counselor told me it had to be an SSN." My mom told me that I don't have one and that none of us have one. I was like I need it. "Can we go get it somewhere?" She said that if they could, they would have done that.

Jackie was confused why no one had told her that she was undocumented. She was ashamed that she did not know. "I didn't know what to think or even say to anyone. I was scared." Like Julia, Jackie did have a pending immigration application. However, she was unsure if the application was still valid as it was filed when she was a minor.

> My father has an immigration case. I am under my dad. It is sibling to sibling for him. My uncle requested my dad. So, we are under my dad. They filed over 10 years ago. It depends on what age you were when they filed. I think. Hopefully I will be covered.

Jackie was hopeful that her status would change in the near future. She graduated in spring 2010 and was eager to receive permission to work.

The DREAM Act or my getting married would help too. I have been with my boyfriend for like four years. We have been thinking about getting married. He's a citizen. I hope to be changing my status in the next few years.

Being an undocumented college student

Jackie's entire educational career took place in the US. Her parents enrolled her in a pre-kindergarten program at age three. She then transitioned to the local elementary school. Her school district offered parents English-only or bilingual instruction. Jackie's parents enrolled her in the bilingual class. "When I was in elementary school, I only spoke in Spanish and read in Spanish …. I was doing Spanish until third or fourth grade. Then [my parents] switched me to English." Jackie did not have any problems learning English. "I always have felt comfortable with English …. My older brothers and sister—well, they struggled more than I did." She attended a total of two elementary schools, one middle school, and one high school. "I was lucky that things were stable because my parents stayed in places a long time."

Even though Jackie was an above average student during elementary and middle school, she never gave much thought to continuing her education past high school. She was intent on receiving a high quality education but was unaware of any postsecondary opportunities. "I knew that I wanted to get a better education so that's when I let my parents send me to the high school my brothers attended in my old neighborhood so I could go to a better high school." She wanted to make the best of her high school experience.

> I think in 9th grade, I really wanted to do something. I noticed that some people … they had the same class … they were together each period. So I would ask them why they were always together. They told me about the program AVID. So, I took the initiative to ask my English teacher—she was the AVID teacher, too. I told her that I wanted to be in the program. She looked at my grades and she was like okay. The next term, I was in AVID.

Joining AVID provided Jackie, like Monica, an entirely different high school experience. She was immersed in a college-going environment where every student was expected to enroll in college. "My family had no expectations for me to go to college. I am the first to go .... AVID was crazy because everyone was going to go to college. I wanted to go too."

Jackie credited AVID for preparing her for college. She was eligible to apply to both the UC and CSU as well as private schools. She planned on using financial aid to help pay for college. "The only thing I worried about was my family—I would have to convince them that I could both go to school and continue to work and help out .... I didn't know then I wouldn't qualify for financial aid." Devastated by the news she was undocumented, Jackie distanced herself from her AVID instructor. She told everyone that she would was not going to attend college because she had a job.

> When I told my AVID teacher the real reason, she was like, "Oh." She understood but she didn't know what to do. She pretty much said that she never had this before and this is a lesson for her to check next time and to screen the students more to make sure that they have one. She didn't help me out. She just left me alone. She understood but she didn't help me figure it out. She focused on the other students. At the time, I was like sure. I felt so guilty … like I wasted her time. I understood.

Jackie did find her way to college the next year. She met a community college admissions representative at her school's college center in May of 12th grade. The representative encouraged Jackie to enroll in community college since she would qualify for reduced fees via AB 540.

> She kept bugging me. And I am like, "I told you lady, I have a job. I already know what I am going to do." Finally, I was just like … "this is my situation. Stop, leave me alone!" …. I told her I wanted to go [to college]. She sat down with me and we went over the whole application. I got my transcript. I plugged it in. I got the printout, signed in, and mailed it in. She told me to go to the school with my official transcript. I started class a week after I graduated.

After enrolling in community college classes, Jackie explained to her parents that she would work a full-time job, limiting her enrollment to evening, weekend, and online courses. She did not plan to transfer. "I was doing part-time .... I joined a club. I was president of the Latino Student Union .... I would go to the different workshops and their forums and panels. I went to their plays and stuff. I liked it."

Jackie transferred to Metro U. after attending community college for four years. "I wasn't going to transfer until I met my boyfriend ... who had just graduated from [a UC campus]." He encouraged Jackie to transfer and helped her create a transfer plan.

> I was paying for school through my job .... We set up a budget because this whole time I was at community college, I actually got two jobs .... I saved $10,000 in two years .... I file taxes so I got refunds, too. He told me to talk to a counselor that got me on track to transfer.

Jackie's boyfriend provided her with both the confidence and the practical information to continue her education. She approached her family with her plans and gained their support.

> I needed their support .... When I graduated [from community college, my parents] were like she is serious, this is what she wants to do. I told my dad that I would need his help. I was going to quit my job and go to school full-time. At first, he was like, "Why are you going to do that? You are making more money than I am. How are we going to make the rent?" I was like, "It will work out. I need my money to go to school." Luckily, that's when my sister moved in because of the divorce. She was able to take over the money I gave.

Jackie's experience at Metro U. had been fulfilling and busy. She regularly participated in the campus's political science club. She also joined the campus's Model United Nations delegation. "I have traveled that way with the school, so I feel comfortable going on a plane in a big group." Jackie joined the campus undocumented student club during her junior year and was elected president her senior year. "I am able to be involved on campus because I saved money for school. I haven't worried too much about how I was going to pay for school like the other students." Jackie graduated at the end of the 2009–2010 academic year as planned.

Life outside of school
Jackie spent a considerable amount of time with her boyfriend. They primarily spent their time developing their online business and cooking. "We are both going to be unemployed once I graduate so I hope to earn some income from the business." Jackie regularly socialized with her friends and family on the weekends. "I keep in touch with some high school and [community college] friends. Sometimes we go to happy hour."

Manny
Manny was a thin and youthful looking 19-year-old sophomore engineering student at Metro U. He made an effort to appear older—he kept a moustache, wore black-rimmed glasses, and usually wore khakis and a button-down madras shirt. "People think I am really young so I try to look more professional." He was particularly thin so his clothes were always too big. Manny's most noticeable physical trait was his ever-present smile. "People always comment on my smile because I guess I am always smiling." Manny was very approachable, always ready to engage in conversation. He hinted that he suffered from bouts of depression. "I get overwhelmed sometimes but I think that it is all normal at my age. I am starting to learn about who I am and what I am going to be as an adult."

Family life
Manny lived with his parents and four younger siblings in a small two-bedroom, one-bathroom apartment about 15 miles distance from Metro U. He had three brothers age nine, seven, and two, as well as one sister who was five years old. The seven-year-old brother was autistic and required constant supervision. His home life was stressful mainly because of the family's living conditions. The apartment was dilapidated and cluttered with the family's possessions. Clothing hung from the bedroom doorways and shelves containing his father's construction tools and children's toys lined the walls.

> Me and my brother have a [clothes] dryer in our bedroom ....
> My dad has extra cars to store stuff in .... We don't even have

room for the cereal so my father figured out that we could put it in grocery bags and hang them from the ceiling, above the kitchen table. My autistic brother sleeps on a shelf behind my parents' bed so they can watch him .... It's stressful living like this.

Manny relationship with his family was "close." He credited their close relationship to being a traditional Mexican family. "You can say that in a Mexican family, we are very close. So, usually it is that the man works and supports the family financially .... That's how it is in my family. We stay together and help each other." As with Julia and Luz, Manny had particularly defined responsibilities within the family. "As the eldest, I have to help with the kids and babysit. I help my mom clean and keep things organized. I have given my father money in the past but I try to just use that for school." Manny regularly translated for his parents. He was also involved in coordinating his autistic brother's care. "[My parents] expect a lot from me and I am able to help so it's good for me."

Since Manny started college in fall 2008, his relationship with his family had changed. "I don't know ... I never thought it would get to me ... everything in the house ... but it has. I just don't want to be [at home] all of the time." Their relationship had changed largely because Manny's parents did not understand what attending college entailed.

I get mad sometimes because [my mother] says that I am getting lazy and I am not helping her as much as before—like around the house and with the kids. But, she doesn't know what I am doing. Sometimes I tell her that she doesn't know me anymore .... She knows that I work now and have a job but she doesn't know the details of what I do all day. This has created some discomfort.

He confessed that he had started to resent him parents for their decisions to have a large family. "I don't understand it now that I am older .... I question their choices." He worried about the increased tension and how it would affect his adult life.

I want to be an example for the younger kids. I feel that if I have to leave my parents in order to do what I have to do in school … then that's something that I have to deal with. It's a must. Because I have to give some things in order to gain others. If it means losing my parents' support for a while but succeeding in something else, then I am okay with it. It's sort of bad …. I sort of feel guilty about this.

Socioeconomic standing

Manny's family's socioeconomic status was "good" compared to some of his peers. "I would say our socioeconomic standing in the US to be good. But, I don't know the details of how much money my dad makes and stuff." He periodically worked a part-time job. "I use my money for school mostly." Manny's father was the sole breadwinner, working construction jobs at local hotels. His mother was a homemaker. Manny's parents both finished primary school in Mexico. His mother had periodically enrolled in adult school, working towards completing her GED. The family received government-issued food and medical benefits to help feed and care for his U.S.-born siblings. His brother received extra public assistance because of his disorder. "Our financial situation has changed over the years. Now … I see that [my parents are] having small troubles once in a while."

Manny's family had lived conservatively for the past 13 years since they had immigrated to the US. They changed apartments only once since they arrived. "We had a place to live when we arrived and then we moved to the apartment I live in now—for the last 13 years." Manny's family did not move because of the relative affordability of the apartment and its location. "I live mostly around Hispanics and African Americans so my parents can speak Spanish here …. The public transportation is good in this area." Manny acknowledged that his neighborhood was unsafe. "I am concerned about the safety issues in my neighborhood because there's violence with the gangs." Since attending Metro U., Manny had started to draw comparisons between his classmates and himself. "Now I can see how [my family] could be [considered] poor. But I didn't know that until I saw other people from other areas and could compare."

Immigration status

Manny immigrated to the US from Mexico with his parents when he was six years old. As with the other students profiled in this study, his family immigrated for better economic and educational opportunities.

Manny did not remember the details of their journey but he did know that they did not have legal permission to travel to the US. He hoped that the circumstances surrounding his immigration—his young age and inability to stay in Mexico—would help his chances of gaining U.S. residency. "I don't want anything bad that will affect when I apply in the future. One day, I want to apply for residency." Manny's siblings were all U.S. citizens. His parents would have the eldest U.S.-born son sponsor them when he turned 21. "I could have him request me, too, but that's 12 years until he turns 21 and then another 10 or 15 years before they review my application. That's a long time." Similar to Luz, Manny had worked on immigration reform in the past. "I hope a law passes like the DREAM Act or something that makes it easier to apply for citizenship or something that bridges the gap between me and citizenship."

Similar to Cristina and Jackie, Manny was unaware of his immigration status until high school.

> I knew that I was an immigrant but I didn't know what *undocumented immigrant* [emphasis added] meant …. I didn't know I was undocumented until I was in 11th grade. I wasn't aware until I was a junior and the seniors started graduating. I saw people having trouble going to college and paying for school and they were not getting financial aid. I got a small sense about how being undocumented affects you.

Manny never adopted a strict insider/outsider mentality. Rather, he considered himself a Hispanic student living in the US.

> I feel that I am a divided person. Because of the fact that I don't know where to place myself, I am taken out of a particular category. I am always in the middle. I am always looking at all of the sides that I am confronting. I try to think about the immigrant thing. I try to look at the news and stuff in a way that it would benefit everyone here in the US. By changing the law it would benefit all of us …. My status is not everything to me …. Even though I will not be able to work, I am hoping that there will be some changes. I am just going to stay with it. I am not going to let anything get me off of my train.

<u>Being an undocumented college student</u>
Manny began elementary school in first grade and enrolled in English-only classes. "I was never really in ESL .... I learned English pretty quickly. I don't have an accent. I just fit in." As with Stephanie's and Alejandra's mothers, Manny's mother played an important role in his education.

> My mom was very involved with me during elementary and middle school. I would come home and she would tell me that I am going to Saturday school. Or, I would go to summer school. I would go to different after-school programs. I would go to community programs that focused on math and physical activities .... She wanted me to do all of those things.

Manny's mother sought advice from his teachers and counselors about his educational opportunities. "I believe this is partly why I was accepted into the magnet program in middle school ... and went to college."

Manny decided to attend college in ninth grade while his brother was being diagnosed with autism. "When they started to diagnose him, I wanted to know what autism was and work on ways to help people like him." His father immediately supported him in his goals, pledging that he would help him in any way possible. "It's ironic because my mom was always the one who supported me in school and then my father told me to continue with it. It was great to know they supported me even if they didn't understand what it meant." Manny was identified as college-bound by his school. "My parents never knew anything about college. I really found out [about college] through my friends in high school who were going to college. Teachers were talking about it. And the counselors expected us to go."

Manny prepared as an undocumented student like many of the students in this study. Similar to Julia, Manny and his friends founded a campus support group for undocumented students. "We would fundraise for application fees and for scholarships .... We also talked about how to make strategic decisions about college .... We shared scholarship info." This group provided Manny with the opportunities to get to know older students who were also undocumented and attending college. Before his senior year began, he knew undocumented students attending many of the local and state universities. "I learned from the older students about what to do. I knew about the money problems and the struggles I would have …. I knew about AB 540 and community college." Manny also took advantage of the handful of teachers who supported the group. "I could ask them for recommendations and advice."

Manny applied to a total of three institutions and myriad undocumented student scholarships. All of the campuses were close to his home and had an established campus undocumented student support group. Before he decided to enroll at Metro U., he spent some time on campus and researched the engineering programs. He also befriended an admissions representative who helped him learn about the campus.

> The rep gave me a personal tour of the campus and he introduced me to the payment plan, the undocumented student support group, and introduced me to the club's two presidents. That's how I became involved with the support group. He also introduced me to one of the advisors in my engineering department …. I also found out about the [campus undocumented student] scholarship.

Manny's pre-enrollment experiences at Metro U. along with its low fees convinced him that Metro U. was the best choice. "I got enough scholarship money to pay for the first year and [my girlfriend] could help with the transportation when I couldn't take the bus …. I started in fall 2008."

Manny's postsecondary experience had been "challenging." He took a full course load his first year but only made a dent in his requirements due to requisite remedial courses. He started taking his major prerequisite courses during his second year but found them challenging. Manny started to think that he might be better suited for another type of job related to autism research. "I think that maybe I should switch my major to communication disorders and not biomedical engineering …. I am good with my brother and I have patience. Maybe I can be a speech pathologist?"

During the 2009–2010 academic year, Manny pondered his academic options. He also ran out of scholarship money before the academic year commenced. "For fall 2009, I had to borrow money from my high school counselor to pay the fees before the deadline. My dad paid her once he got money." He started working in summer 2009 to pay for his academic fees. "I have been working at an afterschool program that my brother goes to and it's great because they know that I am undocumented and they still wanted to hire me." Manny's father contributed to his school expenses and his girlfriend helped out when she had extra money. "The fees are getting higher and I can't participate in the undocumented group anymore because I have to leave in the afternoon to work."

> Manny decided to take a leave of absence starting fall 2010.
> I am taking academic leave from [Metro U.] so that I can attend community college for a while. I decided to attend [community college] because I have received my job back at the afterschool program … and I wanted to be close to where I work. I plan to take general ed courses while at [a community college] and possibly other classes that have caught my attention.

Attending community college would allow him to finish his major preparation courses and save money for two final years at Metro U. "I am not getting off course. I am taking another route to finish my goals."

Life outside of school
Manny's life outside of school centered around his family and girlfriend. His girlfriend would come over to the apartment and spend time with his family. They would take care of his younger siblings and watch movies. They also studied at the library. Manny worked approximately 15 hours per week. He also helped his younger siblings with their homework. He struggled to keep up with his household responsibilities as work, school, and extracurricular activities took more of his time. "I find myself doing more stuff on the weekends to catch up …. I keep busy. I always have something to do."

THE METRO U. CONTEXT
A discussion of how undocumented Metro U. students interacted with one another and the types of activities they undertook is helpful to more thoroughly complete the analysis necessary to answer the project's research questions. Spending the entire academic year on campus, I was exposed to a variety of events Metro U. students organized and supported. Most of the on- and off-campus events students participated

in were facilitated by IMAGINE—Metro U.'s undocumented student support group. The group organized weekly meetings, fundraisers, and community outreach events, which the nine profiled Metro U. students regularly attended. The 16 other Metro U. students I interviewed also attended these gatherings.

This section highlights three such events that took place during the academic year—the fall 2009 IMAGINE open house, the March 2010 statewide budget cuts action day protest, and a February 2010 weekly IMAGINE meeting. I chose to highlight these three events for a couple of reasons. First, many of the study participants attended these if not similar events throughout the year. These events are representative of typical academic, political, and social gatherings where undocumented Metro U. students gathered. Second, these events, especially the statewide budget cuts action day, are indicative of the types of opportunities undocumented Metro U. students had to advocate on their own behalf on and off campus. In the process, they were able to identify as undocumented immigrants with little fear of legal repercussions. Now I turn to a description of each of the three events.

IMAGINE Fall Open House
It was about 5:45 p.m. on a Thursday evening in early October 2009. The double doors leading to the City Room in the Metro U. Student Union were decorated with balloons and IMAGINE posters. A group of about 75 students, parents, and young children lingered in the hallway around the door, waiting for registration to begin. Luz, the junior sociology major and IMAGINE's vice president, and a few other students were setting up the registration table. One IMAGINE member stood guard by the door, answering students' questions and assuring attendees that the open house would begin shortly. Manny was in a corner of the hallway, holding hands with his girlfriend. Monica, the 22-year-old sociology major and the group's fundraising chair, was coordinating the food delivery from a local Italian restaurant. At 6:00 p.m., Jackie, the IMGAINE president, opened the double doors signaling the beginning of registration. The fall 2009 IMAGINE Open House formally commenced.

IMAGINE hosted an open house at the beginning of each term. For fall 2009, the group planned a larger event scheduled in the evening so that members of the community could attend. The open house had three primary objectives: (a) provide information about IMAGINE's mission and activities, (b) inform prospective and current Metro U. undocumented students about general and campus-specific information regarding undocumented student issues and support services, and (c) provide a forum for local organizers to discuss their immigration-related activism at the local, state, and national levels. The group received $1,200 from the Metro U. student government to host and cater the event. Approximately 100 Metro U. students, staff, and faculty as well as community organizers, local high school students, and students' families attended the event.

Jackie and Luz led the meeting. All presentations were simultaneously conducted in English and Spanish so that all attendees could understand. Jackie and Luz focused on the group's fundraising, outreach, and scholarship opportunities. They shared details about how they each arrived at Metro U., one as a transfer student and the other as a freshman. They also explained the daily struggles they encountered as college students. Jackie focused on the challenges she encountered convincing her family that pursuing a college education was worthwhile. Luz stressed the importance of having a support system of college peers that inspired her to persevere. Members of the board, including Monica, also joined the presentation, describing their outreach, scholarship, and fundraising goals for the academic year. They encouraged Metro U. undocumented students to join as they would benefit from the support and camaraderie of the group.

The next three presentations featured a Metro U. admissions officer, a Metro U. professor, and a community organizer with a statewide immigration coalition. The admissions representative outlined the basic tenets of AB 540. He answered questions from high school students and their parents about the legislation and its availability at all California public postsecondary institutions. He then detailed the current efforts of the Metro U. administration to open campus-specific scholarships to undocumented students. A Metro U. political science professor spoke next regarding the ongoing federal immigration reform legislation. She drew comparisons with past efforts to expand civil rights to marginalized groups. The professor also detailed the efforts of some of her colleagues who focused on providing more financial and academic resources to campus undocumented students. Finally, the community organizer discussed the efforts by student, labor, and educational activists to pass the federal DREAM Act. She fielded questions about how undocumented immigrants and their allies could help in the effort to pass immigration reform. The event concluded with a general question and answer forum on undocumented immigrant-related topics.

IMAGINE members declared the event a success. The open house served as both a recruitment and community outreach event; Metro U. undocumented students showcased the club's activities and support services, and provided current information about undocumented immigrant issues affecting the larger off-campus community. Julia, the freshman who co-founded an undocumented student support group at her high school, was particularly pleased that the open house both targeted the campus and surrounding communities.

> Americans have this stereotypical view of the undocumented people ... they are the garment workers, they are the sales workers, they don't speak English, they don't go to school, they are not educated, they just came here to do the dirty jobs .... They don't want to integrate [into] the community .... You see at these types of events that people do want to learn about what they can do and how they can better themselves .... [Americans] don't know that we want a better life. We want to work. We want to better ourselves. We also want to participate in the economic section of the country. We want to contribute to the country.

Stephanie, the recent transfer student and 2010–2011 IMAGINE president, shared that the open house was particularly useful for the high school students in attendance. "Showing [younger] students that success is possible is critical. If I see that someone else is succeeding, I will at least try." She planned on organizing similar events during her tenure as president. Other members who were unable to attend due to their class and work schedules commented that their friends thought that the event was a success. Cristina, the junior Spanish major regretted not attending. "There were a lot of people. I could have let the people at my old community college know about it. I just didn't know about IMAGINE that early in the year."

March 2010 Budget Cuts Action Day
Another event that lends context to the environment where Metro U. interviewees pursued their academic goals was the March 2010 budget

cuts rally and protest. The 2009–2010 academic year was plagued by unprecedented statewide education budget cuts. Metro U. student, staff, and faculty anti-budget and union groups formed a campus-wide coalition opposing the drastic cutbacks. On March 4, the Metro U. No Budget Cuts Coalition organized a day of budget-related events aimed at educating the campus community of the reduced budget's effects on public education. The campus rally took place from 8:00 a.m. to 2:00 p.m. and included a campus-wide class walkout, speakers, and a march across campus. The event ended with students, staff, and faculty boarding city buses en route to a larger regional education budget cuts rally. Campus, city, and state law enforcement patrolled the Metro U. event, accompanying demonstrators to the larger regional rally.

Eight of the nine profiled Metro U. students participated in the day's on- and off-campus events. One student chose not to participate due to the large police presence and possibility of arrests. There was serious debate during several IMAGINE meetings about whether the group should officially co-sponsor the event. Monica questioned the feasibility of the larger campus student groups controlling their memberships in case of civil disobedience. "How do we know that someone in their group is not just going to throw something at the cops and get us all arrested?" Cristina was concerned that the event was not safe to attend. "I don't think that this is a good idea …. There's going to be police and cameras and … I don't need my family seeing me on TV. They're already concerned that I am part of [IMAGINE]." Alejandra, having frequently marched and protested due to her involvement with other grassroots organizations, offered a possible solution for concerned IMAGINE members who wanted to attend the rally. "The nonprofit I work with, we bring lawyers with us. We stand next to them and never leave them …. If the *pigs* [police] try to arrest us, we have our lawyers right there. We can walk with them."

Given the debate surrounding the safety of undocumented students attending the budget coalition events, Metro U. undocumented student participation was sizeable. A total of eight undocumented Metro U. students participated in the campus rally. A former IMAGINE student member, was a featured speaker. He discussed the impact of the budget cuts on undocumented students attending Metro U. "I am not undocumented anymore but those who are don't get financial aid. They can't ask for emergency loans …. They get no support from administration to pay their fees. They are completely ignored in this debate." Others held signs and participated in the class walkout and campus march. Alba, the undecided freshman, led a group of her friends in anti-budget cut chants. "I see that people don't support the budget cuts. It's wrong for everyone." Cristina stopped by and watched the crowd from the back. She was pleased to see a variety of Metro U. community members—faculty, staff, and students—participating in the campus rally. "It shows that it's not just the students who care about the fees and what's happening to our public education."

Metro U. rally organizers provided city bus tokens for those who wanted to attend the regional rally. Monica, Stephanie, Alba, Jackie, and Luz boarded the city buses along with approximately 250 other Metro U. participants. Seven more Metro U. undocumented students joined the group at the regional rally. The IMAGINE students held up posters displaying pro-AB 540 messages. Monica was asked by a German film crew to explain her AB 540 sign and why she was protesting.

> We are undocumented immigrants who are going to college. AB 540 lets us pay the less expensive in-state fees …. These budget cuts are threatening to informally bar us from our rights to an education. We are being priced out of our education.

Jackie was excited to see that so many students and educators participated in the rally. "I should have brought my little sister and my nieces. They could see that their teachers do care about the cuts and want to fight for them." The rally ended at 7:00 p.m. without any reported arrests.

The Metro U. and regional rallies marked the first time some of the Metro U. undocumented students marched or protested in large-scale events. Alba was surprised at the number of attendees who participated in the regional rally. "I was still in high school when the May 2006 immigration rallies happened. My parents wouldn't let me go then. It was amazing that all of these people showed up." Alejandra was less surprised by the regional rally turnout. "I do this type of stuff all of the time. People are angry and that's when they come out and scream and wave banners and stuff. They come out yelling for their human rights." Stephanie was happy with the outcome of the on- and off-campus rallies and protests. "[The undocumented] are coming out and letting people know that we cannot and will not stand for this abuse .... We stand in solidarity with all of the other citizens and immigrants who are being punished for politicians' mistakes."

The March 4 day of action showed many Metro U. undocumented students that diverse segments of society did in fact care about public education funding. After her interview with the German film crew, Monica explained that she was heartened to know that people outside of the US were not only concerned with general access to education but also the plight of undocumented immigrants. "After I gave the interview, I was shocked that these people would even care about undocumented immigrants going to college .... I don't know if they were serious but the questions they asked—at least they asked them." Jackie felt that the rallies were revealing insofar as she saw diverse people talking about the same issue—saving public education.

> When I saw the IMAGINE students standing next to the arts teachers and the teachers unions and the students themselves, demanding that funding be restored to the public schools, I was impressed .... People tend to see these issues as only supported by a certain type of person. The reality is that it is just common sense to support education.

The Metro U. campus initially planned to hold another budget cuts rally on campus later in the year. That rally would also include local primary and secondary school students. IMAGINE members did not participate in that event as it was on the weekend and students had prior commitments.

A Weekly IMAGINE Meeting
Weekly IMAGINE meetings were a regular place for Metro U. interviewees to mingle and meet other campus undocumented students. Meetings were held every Thursday during the campus's daily mid-afternoon break so as to maximize student attendance. Weekly attendance ranged from 10 to 35 students. Meetings were held in a student union conference room. The meeting agenda was usually projected onto a video screen. Individual introductions were followed by updates on recurring and upcoming events and activities. Different board members reported on the events they organized and led. For instance, the high school committee presentation chair provided

updates on future high school and regional AB 540 financial aid presentations. As the fundraising chair, Monica detailed the upcoming campus fundraisers and asked for volunteers to staff the events. After group business was settled, campus groups made topical presentations. Student government candidates introduced themselves to the group on one occasion. Another week, an EOP counselor updated the group on spring 2010 class registration and counseling services. Meetings ended promptly at 4:15 p.m. as most students hurried off to their late-afternoon classes.

In the middle of the school year, the IMAGINE board decided to add an immigration-related discussion to the weekly meeting. Jackie explained that the board was concerned about waning attendance at meetings. "We're all stressed out about money. Some of us are working more than before. We have to make these meetings more interesting for the members so that they come and not just walk out after the announcements." Jackie announced in early February that the group would facilitate weekly discussions on immigration issues during future meetings.

The February 25 meeting marked the beginning of member-initiated weekly immigration discussions. The start of the meeting included member introductions, an update on a local high school AB 540 presentation, a presentation for an upcoming 18-mile immigration reform awareness fundraiser walk, and the year-end IMAGINE graduation celebration. Stephanie then led a discussion about Princess Hijab, an anonymous street artist working in Paris, France. Her street art centers on painting a black hijab—a traditional headscarf worn by Muslim women—on models featured in subway advertisements. Stephanie chose to speak about Princess Hijab due to the ongoing debate in France regarding the influx of Muslim immigrants living in the country.

> I want to talk about Princess Hijab and how the artist is bringing the reality of xenophobia in regards to immigrants to the forefront of the French people …. One of the first things you see when you are commuting to work or school in the morning is a hijab painted on a Western- or French-looking model on a billboard. You can't ignore something like that. In my opinion, it's like if a tagger climbed up on a billboard here and wrote "illegal immigrant" on random models. You have to

stop and think in both cases why these *foreign invaders*
[emphasis added] like Muslims or Mexicans are living in your
country now …. Society has to think about the reasons why
people leave their homes—like colonialism or NAFTA or
neoliberal policies—and make a new home in a new country.
Princess Hijab is doing that with his or her art.

Stephanie's presentation started a lively discussion about
immigration trends, immigration reform, and personal freedoms both in
the US and abroad. Alejandra shared that Princess Hijab's street art was
an effective way to start a discussion about immigrants living in France
and the US.

I wish we had someone here tagging up the freeways and
walls with stuff that matters like this. This has a higher
meaning and sends a message to all people who see it …. You
don't need to be informed like we are to have a reaction.
That's the point. People in France see this and either like it or
hate it for whatever reasons …. We should have an artist like
this making us think as we go to work and school in the
morning.

Jackie agreed with a few other students who thought the art was
possibly confusing the separate issues of immigration and religion. "I
think it's confusing what Princess Hijab is doing …. There's intentions
there that none of us know about. Yeah, maybe the artist just wants to
cover up the models in the ads with conservative clothing?" The
conversation continued after the meeting among some students who did
not have class.

IMAGINE meetings were an opportunity for Metro U.
undocumented students to discuss their opinions about immigration-
related issues openly and honestly. Students could draw on their own
personal experiences as undocumented immigrants to inform their
arguments and positions. Julia was relieved that such a forum was
available on campus.

In my classes, I sometimes have to think about who is around
before I say something. I always try to figure out who is for
the undocumented immigrants and who is against them when I

am in classes. That way I know if I can be more honest about
my opinions.

Other students shared similar sentiments about the importance of
weekly IMAGINE meetings. Cristina appreciated the opportunity to be
herself at the meetings. "I just know that the IMAGINE people are
undocumented and that's it. I don't have to ask them or pick up on their
hints or stuff. I know that many of them are undocumented or were
undocumented." Luz, an IMAGINE member since high school,
summarized the important role IMAGINE had played in her own
education.

> We're family and that's it. We take care of each other. These
> are my friends and … we do stuff together that's serious and
> fun …. They support me like my mom and sister do and I
> never forget their help and strength. I have been coming [to
> IMAGINE meetings and events] since high school and I have
> always felt that this is my home …. These students are my
> friends. It's good to know they are here for me.

CHAPTER SUMMARY
The data presented in this chapter delineates how Metro U.
undocumented students prepare and attend a four-year postsecondary
institution. Their ability to attend college is shaped by such things as
familial responsibilities, primary and secondary educational
experiences, and perceptions of their immigration status and its
limitations. No two students were alike in their progression towards
enrollment at Metro U. Each student prepared for postsecondary
enrollment using different resources. Each found inspiration in various
aspects of their lives. I now turn to a discussion focusing on the study's
primary research questions and results.

CHAPTER FIVE

Conclusion: Making Sense of the Data

The purpose of this study has been to understand how undocumented students created personal and communal identities that fostered the development of class-based social capital that in turn helped them attend four-year institutions. The study explored how these students:

- conceptualized themselves within the undocumented immigration debate,
- identified themselves among other low-income and first-generation students, and
- shaped their educational goals working within a system that did not guarantee their access to a postsecondary education.

These processes occurred within a societal context that simultaneously negated and supported their presence in the United States; they were guaranteed a K–12 education as children yet they were barred from full participation in society as they transitioned to adulthood. This study aimed to explain how undocumented college students attending one institution—Metropolitan University (Metro U.)—viewed, interpreted, and experienced these contradictory realities while pursuing their educational goals.

As the data in the previous chapter show, undocumented Metro U. students arrived at college by different methods and with varying means. Some transferred to Metro U., while others began their postsecondary studies at the institution. The majority struggled to pay for college while a minority relied on ample savings or parental contributions. A few students were knowledgeable about how to attend college as undocumented immigrants while others were relatively ignorant about the subject. Thus, there was no one archetype of a Metro U. undocumented student. By examining the familial, socioeconomic, immigration, and educational experiences of Metro U. students, this study provided a more nuanced portrait of how such students actually attended a four-year institution.

This final chapter provides an analysis of the data presented in Chapter 4. I start the chapter with a brief review of the difficulties undocumented students encounter when they pursue a college education. I then revisit the basic tenets of social capital theory. I provide an explanation as to why I employed the theory in examining how students overcome such challenges. I outline the qualitative methods used in this study before explaining its primary limitations. Next, I discuss the study's findings including the three main themes that emerged from the data within a context of social capital theory. I then answer the study's four questions. Finally, I advance possible theoretical and practical implications of the study's findings on future research concerning undocumented students.

UNDOCUMENTED STUDENTS AND SOCIAL CAPITAL THEORY

Undocumented college students encounter significant barriers in finishing a postsecondary degree. Most hail from low-income households and are the first in their families to attend college. A review of the relevant literature indicates that many undocumented students encounter similar types of problems when pursuing a college education. These impediments usually fall into one of three general areas— financial obstacles, academic preparation, and perceptions of belonging.

The majority of undocumented college students struggle to pay for their college education. Undocumented students are ineligible for federal and state financial aid (Perez et al., 2009); thus, they generally pay out of pocket for their education. In the case of Metro U., California Assembly Bill 540 (AB 540) provides eligible students access to reduced in-state academic fees. As noted in Chapters 2 and 4, AB 540 amounts to some relief but is in no way a substitution for access to traditional federal and state financial aid programs. Employment restrictions on undocumented immigrants further complicate students' financial situations. Most of these students do not have legal permission to work in the US. Students typically find off-campus jobs concentrated in the low-paying service industry (Hermes, 2008; Perez et al., 2009; Suarez-Orozco & Suarez-Orozco, 2001). Students are also foreclosed from most private academic scholarships, stipends, and sponsorships due to their immigration status. In short, undocumented students face formidable obstacles when financing their education.

Academic preparation is another hurdle for undocumented students transitioning to college. First, undocumented students often attend low-performing, ethnically-isolated schools located in urban and inner-city communities (Gandara, 1995; Gonzales, 2009; Teranishi & Briscoe, 2006). Students' college readiness is not only determined by the rigor of high school coursework but also their English language skills (Adelman, 1996, 1998, 2006). These schools usually do not adequately prepare undocumented students for college-level coursework. Also, undocumented students, as first-generation college students, rely more on institutional actors for comprehensive college information (Gonzales, 2009; Perez et al., 2009; Stanton-Salazar, 1997). Their limited access to some college preparation programs affects their preparation for postsecondary study. Thirdly, scholars have found that some undocumented students experience a sense of despair during their educational careers, withdrawing from school coursework and activities (Gonzalez et al., 2003; Suarez-Orozco & Suarez-Orozco, 2001). These students are less prepared for college-level coursework, with some foregoing their postsecondary goals altogether.

The third obstacle that students encounter concerns their perceptions of belonging in the US as undocumented immigrants. Scholars explain that many undocumented students lose their sense of belonging fostered by their inclusion in K–12 schooling as they transition to adulthood (Abrego, 2006; Lopez, 2003). Further, feeling "included" in academic settings is important to student success (Allen & Solorzano, 2001; Blackwell, 1981; Contreras, 2009; Hurtado et al., 1999; Perez Huber, 2009). Individual feelings of inclusion are diminished as undocumented students transition from a childhood with guaranteed K–12 education to an adulthood with no educational guarantees. Undocumented students' feelings of inclusion on college campuses are repeatedly under threat since their immigration status is equivalent to illegality (Abrego, 2008). They are constantly reminded that they are different than their college-going peers, officially excluded from the political and social environments they inhabit (Abrego, 2008; Olivas, 2009; Seif, 2004).

The hardships that undocumented college students confront are complex and far-reaching. As chronicled in Chapter 4, the nine Metro U. students experienced some if not all of these types of difficulties. The majority of students consistently struggled to finance their postsecondary studies. Many strove to meet the academic expectations of college-level work while fulfilling other responsibilities and duties. Finally, all of the nine students grappled with what it meant to be an undocumented immigrant pursuing a college education.

Given these and other challenges that students face, I chose social capital theory as the theoretical lens through which I would examine students' experiences. Social capital is the investment in social networks as well as in mutual recognition and acknowledgment. The theory is one way to understand how individuals and networks interact within a specific social structure. As I outlined in Chapter 2, social capital theory explores how individuals and groups access resources through social relationships, and which types of relationships and resources are most conducive to building social capital. The theory is particularly useful in an investigation of how undocumented immigrant students attend college. The theory has been widely used in educational studies as a means to explain differences in educational attainment.

Theorists have promoted two distinct versions of social capital—a "bridging" variety and a "bonding" variety. Bourdieu (1986) describes bridging social capital as the relationships and networks of social relations that link an individual or group to resources outside of one's immediate social circle. Bridging social capital enables actors to build relationships with socially heterogeneous groups that hold different types of resources. Coleman (1988, 1990) describes bonding social capital as consisting of norms and social control. Bonding social capital involves relationships with socially homogeneous groups that maintain the same types of social values and norms. Both types of social capital are beneficial to individuals and groups that use their relations' resources to assist with accomplishing goals.

As I discuss later in this chapter, students' abilities to garner the support of others—namely institutional agents, relatives, and friends— were integral in their successful matriculation. These supporters provided financial, academic, and personal resources that helped Metro U. students prepare for and attend college. Resources and assistance accessed through bridging and bonding social capital were important in overcoming obstacles faced by undocumented college students. Further, students' different social ties—either strong or weak—with other individuals and groups provided opportunities to access resources that directly benefitted their academic careers.

Students' sources of social capital, as described in Chapter 4, constantly evolved to meet their needs. For the majority of students, the mechanics of how they funded their education, commuted to campus, or enrolled in courses changed from term to term. As the Metro U. community responded to unprecedented budget cuts by raising fees and reducing course offerings, students adjusted their work schedules and their degree course plans to continue their studies. They had to access old and new social capital resources to remain enrolled in school. Thus, students were constantly on the lookout for new academic, work, and personal opportunities that would facilitate their educational goals. Their need for reliable social capital sources never diminished. The study's findings demonstrate how influential social capital was in the academic success of the nine Metro U. students. I now turn to a review of the study's design and limitations.

STUDY DESIGN AND LIMITATIONS

Recall in Chapter 3, I chose to employ qualitative methods throughout the duration of the study. Qualitative researchers emphasize the value-laden nature of inquiry, seeking answers to questions that explain how social experience is created and given meaning (Denzin & Lincoln, 2000). This qualitative study focused on the educational experiences and perceptions of current Metro U. undocumented students. Metro U. was the primary site so as to maximize the number of matriculating undocumented student participants recruited through "snowball sampling" (Salganik & Heckathorn, 2004; Watters & Biernacki, 1989). The university is a large, public, comprehensive Hispanic-Serving Institution (HSI) located in a metropolitan area with the nation's largest undocumented immigrant population. The university also has relatively low academic fees—approximately $5,000 per year. Lastly, I chose Metro U. since I had existing ties to undocumented students at the location (Garcia & Tierney, 2011). The study focused on how Metro U. students constructed and enacted their identities as college students in complex learning and living environments. I wanted to learn how undocumented college students developed college-going identities as well as how they persisted in pursuing their postsecondary goals.

I utilized three qualitative methods—participant observations, interviews, and document analysis—to understand how Metro U. students pursued their postsecondary goals. I engaged in two types of participant observation—group and individual—that allowed me to examine students' singular and communal circumstances and experiences. Formal and informal interviews provided an opportunity to inquire about specific student issues and experiences. The formal interviews relied on a semi-structured interview protocol that targeted students' family-, education-, immigration-, and social-related experiences. Informal interviews occurred during group and individual observations and provided for follow-up and clarification of data. Finally, document analysis provided context and background for the data collected during observations and interviews. I regularly reviewed immigration-related articles and reports from both mainstream news outlets and academic research centers. I also reviewed documents, news, and announcements posted on the IMAGINE—Metro U.'s undocumented student group—online discussion board. All data was collected between September 2009 and June 2010.

The primary limitations of the study are fourfold. The first limitation concerns the relatively small size of the study sample. Metro U. does not collect demographic information sufficient to definitively identify undocumented matriculants. Therefore, it is impossible to know exactly how many undocumented immigrants attend Metro U. Estimated undocumented student populations at neighboring University of California (UC) and California State University (CSU) campuses range from approximately 150 to over 550 students per campus. Given the location of Metro U., it is reasonable to conclude that the sample of 25 Metro U. students represents a small proportion of actual undocumented Metro U. students. Comparing and contrasting the experiences of such a small group of students on the campus affects the applicability of the findings to all undocumented Metro U. students. The homogeneity of the sample—all Metro U. study participants are of Mexican origin—also limits the scope of the findings. For example, undocumented students originating from Asia or Europe may have a different immigration trajectory.

The second limitation involves the retrospective nature of the collected data. Even though I relied on several different methods—observations, interviews, and document analysis—for data collection, most of the data originates from the interviews. Much of what was discussed during the interviews occurred in the distant past. Therefore, it is unclear how students' recollections of events differ from the actual events. This issue is complicated by the emotional nature of the events we explored, such as separating from family members and friends and learning a new language and culture. The emotional recollections students recounted often differed from the actual facts of the matter. Therefore, I regularly asked similar if not the same questions more than once on different occasions to ensure those students were accurately recalling the information. When there were discrepancies, I clarified the issue with students.

The third limitation regards the universality of the study's findings. The results are not wholly applicable to other undocumented immigrant college students matriculating at other institutions. Rather, the findings are unique to the study participants attending Metro U.—a four-year, public, comprehensive university that is situated in a vast metropolitan area with a large and established undocumented immigrant population. Because of immigrants' longstanding presence in the larger community and the passage of AB 540 almost a decade ago, Metro U. undocumented students encountered a small but vocal on-campus community that supported their presence in higher education. This environment allowed Metro U. students to more freely share their immigration status with little fear of institutional sanctions or legal repercussions. As the study's supplementary interviews revealed, not all UC and CSU undocumented students experienced such a welcoming on-campus environment. This study's results are context-bound and only applicable to the Metro U. campus.

The final significant limitation of the study concerns the function of qualitative research itself. My role as researcher affected data collection and interpretation. As a U.S.-born citizen whose entire family consisted of U.S.-born citizens and documented immigrants, I brought my own lens to the research. Even though my surname is

Garcia and my father's family is Mexican, my light phenotype is rarely associated with being Latina in the US. Hence I have not experienced living in the US as a visible minority. My personal experiences differed from those experiences of most of the study participants. I would never know how it felt to be an undocumented Latino living in the US. I tried to remedy these limitations by using verbatim data when possible. I also arranged for a few of the study participants to review parts of Chapter 4 for veracity.

FINDINGS
The data demonstrate that Metro U. undocumented students arrived at their postsecondary education with different experiences, expectations, and plans. There was no one right way to matriculate. This section focuses on my three primary findings or themes about what Metro U. students experienced while pursuing a postsecondary education. The three themes are:

1. Institutional agents were instrumental in developing students' social capital.
2. Family- and peer-based social capital was important to students' matriculation.
3. Perceptions about immigration status affected students' matriculation and social capital development.

The themes emerged from collected data guided by the study's four research questions. The themes incorporate aspects of students' family lives, socioeconomic standing, immigration, and academic experiences. Students' academic success largely depended on their ability to access financial, emotional, and academic resources both inside and outside of their immediate family and peer groups. Acquisition of diverse forms of social capital through both strong and weak ties with institutional agents also contributed to students' success. However, social capital could only get students so far in pursuing their dreams. Their beliefs about how their undocumented immigration status had affected and will affect them in the future influenced students' acquisition of quality social capital. I now turn to a discussion of each theme.

Finding 1: Institutional Agents Were Instrumental in Developing Students' Social Capital

Institutional agents played significant roles in students' preparation and matriculation as undocumented immigrants. As I explain later in this chapter, they helped students locate, acquire, and activate reliable and useful sources of social capital that in turn ensured their success as postsecondary students. Secondary and postsecondary instructors and counselors provided undocumented students with vital and timely information about college options, California's in-state academic fee policy (AB 540), and scholarship opportunities. They helped students get in touch with the respective people and resources that would assist them in their success. Agents regularly extended their support and encouragement to undocumented students pursuing a higher education. Most of the study participants believed that if they had not been influenced by institutional agents to attend college, they likely would not have enrolled at Metro U.

High school agents

Educational practitioners in the high school setting provided undocumented students with opportunities to plan for college in a prudent and efficacious manner. Instructors, counselors, and coaches all played important roles in students' acquisition of social capital related to preparing for college as undocumented immigrants. Recall that Monica, Alejandra, Julia, and Manny all relied on instructors for undocumented-related academic and financial information. Monica's Advancement Via Individual Determination (AVID) Program instructor was extremely helpful in providing her with specialized admissions and financial aid information for undocumented students. He talked to her about AB 540 and undocumented student scholarships. He also strategized with her about her college options. She explained, "He … helped me make practical decisions about where to go." Monica's instructor provided her with a comprehensive and realistic plan about how to approach her college education given her resources. This relationship was an example of bridging social capital; Monica benefitted from the relationship with her instructor as he provided her with relevant and accurate college preparation information unavailable from her relatives and friends. Without this information, she would not have been as well prepared to attend college immediately after high school graduation.

Alejandra also relied on high school instructors for pertinent information about college. She benefitted from her close relationship with her high school teacher who once worked as a UC admissions counselor. He explained how AB 540 worked and also how to become a competitive applicant for undocumented student scholarships. Alejandra's teacher put her in contact with various community and campus organizers who were key in implementing the AB 540-related policies on individual campuses. As a result, Alejandra could access multiple undocumented-friendly postsecondary academic and financial resources during high school and college. Like Monica, Alejandra's bridging relationship with her high school instructor set her on a path of continued access to varied sources of social capital throughout her college career.

Julia and Manny's respective high school instructors provided unique opportunities to build relationships with other undocumented students through the formation of campus undocumented student support groups. This type of social capital permitted both Julia and Manny to not only learn more about their predicament as undocumented immigrants but also be exposed to resources and people that aided students like them in continuing their education. Recall that Julia's membership in her campus's support group was instrumental in her learning about how to attend college as an undocumented immigrant. "We were all looking to go to college. That's what we talked about ... how are we going to [go to college]. We talked about what we needed to do and who we needed to talk to and stuff." This group would not have formed if the school's instructors and counselors did not provide support for the group. Julia relied on an AVID instructor's advice and contacts to build a relationship with a local UC campus undocumented student support group. In addition, her instructors and counselors helped her prepare academically and financially to attend a four-year institution immediately after high school.

One of Manny's high school instructors took an interest in his plans to attend college by helping him gather the resources to start an undocumented student support group. Like Julia, he was able to network with other undocumented students attending his high school. He gained financial and academic advice from older students who were preparing for college and discovering the challenges of matriculation. Manny's own preparation for college benefitted from observing their struggles. He explained, "I learned from the older students about what to do. I knew about the money problems and the struggles I would have …. I knew about AB 540 and community college." Manny also relied on several of his high school instructors to help him prepare for college as an undocumented immigrant. He felt that he was better prepared to enroll at a four-year institution like Metro U. because he had access to college preparation information and resources during his high school career.

High school academic and college counselors also provided students with key information and resources. Luz depended on her college counselor to help her plan to attend college as an undocumented immigrant. Starting in 10th grade, Luz worked with her counselor on finding money and resources that would help her attend college. Luz's counselor encouraged her to attend local financial aid workshops where she met current undocumented college students. These undocumented student contacts at local two- and four-year institutions helped her plan for her education. Further, her new contacts at Metro U. invited her to attend IMAGINE meetings while she was still enrolled in high school. Armed with several bridging social capital resources, Luz was well prepared to transition to Metro U. as a freshman. She partly credited her counselor's assistance in meeting people and accessing academic and financial resources while still in high school for her success in college. She made connections with people outside of her immediate social group during the college preparation process that served her throughout her studies at Metro U.

Alba also benefited from a strong relationship with her high school magnet counselor. Her counselor not only helped her plan for college, she also assisted Luz in acquiring a personal mentor through a local community mentoring program focused on helping first-generation students transition to college. This personal mentor provided Alba with key information about AB 540 and financial opportunities presented at local financial aid seminars. Both the counselor and the mentor provided Alba with opportunities to expand her social capital beyond the traditional resources available to high school students. Alba's mentor helped her secure private scholarship money before she graduated from high school. The mentor remained available to Alba during her first year at Metro U. Alba's counselor provided her access to a relationship with a mentor who possessed various sources of bridging social capital.

Postsecondary agents

Two- and four-year institutional agents were also instrumental in helping study participants achieve their postsecondary goals. Staff members and faculty exposed students to resources and personal contacts that increased students' abilities to locate and access useful social capital. Monica was an example of a student who benefitted from the expertise of a community college staff member. Albeit her relationship with the staff member was relatively weak, this example of bridging social capital proved invaluable to her initial transition to college. Once she enrolled at the local community college, the staff member procured Monica a Board of Governors Waiver (BOGW) that paid her enrollment fees. Monica also was able to access the Extended Opportunity Program & Services (EOPS) resources at her college. Not only did she save money by not having to pay enrollment fees, Monica could access extra counseling and tutoring services as well as priority course enrollment. Monica's staff contact provided her with an opportunity that was usually denied to undocumented students who did not automatically qualify for such programs and services.

Stephanie and Jackie also benefitted from additional social capital as a result of their interactions with community college faculty and staff. Once she enrolled in a local community college, Stephanie became close with several of her professors. She benefitted from their advice regarding her future studies as well as their contacts at Metro U. and other local universities. Stephanie received pertinent academic guidance that she missed as an undocumented student at her high school. Her community college professors helped her transfer to Metro U. Their mentorship and resources proved invaluable to Stephanie who had the academic skills to attend Metro U. but lacked the practical know-how of attending college as an undocumented immigrant.

Jackie's brief, last minute interaction with a community college admissions representative in her high school's college center facilitated her enrollment at a local community college. Her brief meeting with the admissions representative was the first time she heard about AB 540 and other options she had as an undocumented immigrant to continue her education. Jackie acquired relevant information about attending college as an undocumented student from a community college institutional agent visiting her high school. Recall how Jackie unexpectedly applied to college during her only meeting with the representative.

> She sat down with me and we went over the whole application. I got my transcript. I plugged it in. I got the printout, signed in, and mailed it in. She told me to go to the school with my official transcript. I started class a week after I graduated.

Her brief interaction with this college representative provided Jackie with enough resources and information to set her on a path to matriculation that she previously considered impossible. This short-term relationship with a knowledgeable institutional agent yielded more relevant college-going information than her participation in the AVID Program. Such powerful bridging social capital was indicative of how quality resources made the difference in undocumented students attending college.

Other students received support from Metro U. staff members and faculty that directly helped them stay in school. Undocumented students could not normally access the campus's Educational Opportunity Program (EOP) services. However because of IMAGINE's connection with senior EOP counselors, Julia regularly consulted with an EOP counselor who assisted campus undocumented college students. Julia's relationship with the EOP counselor increased her awareness of campus resources and contacts that could help her matriculate. Alejandra's relationships with several sympathetic Metro U. instructors allowed her access to free textbooks and late enrollment in courses. The support she received from Metro U. faculty members helped her remain enrolled in school even during periods of extreme economic hardship. Again, these bridging sources of social capital made the difference in students' abilities to attend Metro U. on a consistent basis.

Finally, Manny received the support of several Metro U. staff members and faculty. His long-standing relationship with a Metro U.

admissions representative and several engineering staff and faculty members led him to acquiring additional campus academic resources helpful to his matriculation. He was introduced to other undocumented students in IMAGINE and his own academic department through these institutional agents. He received emotional support as well as academic supplies like free or discounted textbooks from these institutional agents. Manny believed that Metro U. staff and faculty members were key to his continued success as a college student, even when he took a leave of absence to attend community college. His enduring relationships and contacts provided him with continued access to reliable social capital resources.

The data demonstrate that with the exception of Cristina, all of the students relied on either an individual or select group of institutional agents at their secondary and postsecondary institutions for assistance in college preparation and matriculation. The majority of secondary and postsecondary instructors and staff members were unaware of the presence of undocumented students on campus. Further, they were ignorant about the barriers students confronted as they transitioned to college and the policies and resources that could aid students during their matriculation. The fact that these nine Metro U. students were able to access timely, accurate, and relevant information about attending college as undocumented immigrants was not the norm in their educational settings but rather the exception. These students benefitted from rare, clandestine bridging social capital held by a minority of institutional agents. These agents took the time to learn about undocumented student issues and actively sought out solutions to students' problems.

It is worth noting that while the majority of students received help from various high school agents, less received guidance from postsecondary agents at community colleges or at Metro U. Metro U. students tended to share personal information about their immigration status with institutional agents only after they felt that they could trust them. Students usually confided in those agents that they personally known for some time. Study participants noted that they had spent more time with high school instructors and counselors than they did with their respective postsecondary agents. Thus, they generally disclosed more personal information to high school agents compared to postsecondary agents.

Students' relationships and interactions with institutional agents at the secondary and postsecondary levels regularly provided access to resources and information that they would otherwise not access. These individuals are examples of bridging social capital that students continually relied on for assistance and support. Regardless of the type of relationships students cultivated with these agents, the benefits of accessing social capital outside of their immediate families' and friends' networks were wholly beneficial to their successful pursuit of a postsecondary degree. The next finding mostly focuses on another variety of social capital—bonding relationships.

Finding 2: Family- and Peer-Based Social Capital Was Important to Students' Matriculation

The second theme that emerged from the study data concerned students' relationships with relatives and friends and the respective resources available within these networks. All of the nine Metro U. students pursued their college degrees with varying educational expectations and levels of support from immediate and extended family members as well as friends and peers. These relatives and friends provided important social capital to students who otherwise lacked the financial, emotional, and personal resources to matriculate on a full-time basis. Some relatives supported students by paying full or partial education-related expenses. Other students received emotional support to pursue a postsecondary education from relatives and friends. Most of the students received encouragement to enroll in college from these supporters early in their educational careers. A handful had to prove their abilities to relatives and friends who questioned the feasibility of them attending college. Regardless of the type or level of support Metro U. students received, approving and supportive family members and peers allowed them to pursue their educational goals against the odds.

Parents

Parental support of students' academic goals was important to their success at Metro U. Recall that Cristina's parents were adamant about her attending college from a young age. Even though she and her parents were unaware of how postsecondary education functioned in the US, they never doubted that Cristina would earn an undergraduate degree. Cristina's parents lived in a neighborhood with higher-performing schools that reinforced the college-going culture and expectations they established at home.

It was assumed in my schools that we were going to go to college. Always. At least one class, it was mentioned that we were going to college. "You are here so you can go to college." That was even in the regular classes. We had workshops every other week on college. We had a lot of colleges and universities come out to our school .... My teachers gave us extra credit to go to college fairs and to go visit colleges .... It was always assumed that we would go. The majority of us went. We were made fun of if we didn't pass a class. It wasn't cool to be the kid who failed a class or got a bad grade.

This type of bonding social capital—namely expectations and norms created by homogenous social groups—allowed Cristina to prepare for college without questioning her abilities and resources. Coupled with her parents' ample savings for her college education, Cristina immediately enrolled at a local community college after high school and finished her general education requirements within two years. She then transitioned to Metro U. to complete her bachelor's degree and planned on graduating in two years. She was the only student in the study who relied solely on her parents for all of her educational, living, and personal expenses. Even though Cristina was poorly prepared to transition to a four-year institution as an undocumented immigrant compared to other profiled Metro U. students, her parents' expectations and financial resources allowed her to proceed with her educational goals in a timely fashion.

Unlike Cristina, the majority of students received varying levels of bonding social capital from their families. Financial support varied and depended on the family's available resources at a given time. Recall that Monica's parents gave her money for school expenses early on in her postsecondary career but ceased their support as they struggled to stay employed. Monica's mother, though, demanded that she pursue a higher education.

> My mom always told me that I had to get an education
> because she doesn't want me to go through the same things
> that she had to go through …. She wanted me to have options.
> She has always had high expectations. She would tell me to go
> to college. She has always told me that I have to go.

This expectation along with her parents' initial financial support helped
Monica pursue a postsecondary education. Even when Monica had to
work more hours and forego enrollment in various academic terms to
pay for her education, she felt compelled to finish her degree so as to
fulfill her mother's dreams.

Some parents provided students with other types of support while
they matriculated. Parents commonly provided free room and board to
students who were enrolled in college. They also did not require
students to contribute to other family-related living expenses. Manny's
parents did not expect him to contribute to the household expenses and
instead instructed him to use the money he earned from his job and
scholarships strictly for school expenses. Coupled with his parents'
support of his college plans, Manny felt confident that he would
eventually finish his bachelor's degree. Stephanie's parents also did not
expect her to contribute to household bills. She used her earnings
exclusively for education-related expenses as well as the car she used to
commute to school and work. Her parents also insisted that she
continue her education and earn an advanced postsecondary degree.
Both students credited their parents for helping them remain enrolled in
school by financing their living expenses and creating an expectation
that they attend college.

Parents also provided emotional support to students who were
attending college. Most of the students in the study had their parents'
support when they decided to prepare for college admission during high
school. Alejandra's parents always encouraged her to pursue a college
education regardless of her undocumented status. Alba recounted that
her parents never discouraged her from pursuing a college education.
They stood by her decision and helped her in any way possible. Luz's
mother and father always had high expectations for her academic
career. Luz believed that because they never wavered in their demands
for her to be the first in their family to attend college, she never

questioned her ability to meet their goals. Even Jackie's parents, who were not initially supportive of her decision to attend college, eventually lent their emotional support to her. She believed that her transferring to Metro U. to finish a bachelor's degree was greatly helped when her parents started supporting her goals.

While the majority of Metro U. students received sustained support from their parents throughout their postsecondary studies, some students' parents vacillated in their support. Recall that Manny's mother questioned why he could not help as much around the house caring for his younger siblings since he had enrolled at Metro U. She was not particularly happy that his studies kept him at campus at odd and inconsistent hours depending on his course and study schedules. His mother's support of his postsecondary education wavered as she saw her son grow physically and emotionally apart from the family. Also, Jackie's parents were not supportive of her decision to pursue a bachelor's degree until they witnessed her dedication and hard work in completing an associate's degree at a local community college. Only after Jackie proved her academic ability and her older sister could replace her lost full-time earnings did she gain her parents' full support.

Siblings

Metro U. students also benefitted from support and resources provided by siblings. Older siblings often helped undocumented students overcome barriers in attending college. Julia and Alba benefitted tremendously from the support of older siblings. Julia's older brother contributed financially to the household expenses. Because of his support, she was not expected to help out with household bills. Recall her explanation about how her bother was expected to help her parents financially. "He's the first born son so that was expected from him …. I was lucky because I could just go to college after high school and not have to give my parents a lot of money for rent and bills." Julia's brother also encouraged her to attend a four-year institution at the same time he was working on his lower division requirements at a community college. Julia believed that her brother's financial support and expectations helped her enroll at Metro U. immediately after completing high school.

Similar to Julia's older brother, Alba's older sister contributed to household expenses. Alba recognized that her sister had sacrificed her own education when she left high school before graduating for the betterment of the entire family. Even though their relationship was not as close as Alba would have preferred, she believed that she honored her sister by working hard in school. The resources that Alba's sister provided the family kept Alba at Metro U. Alba knew that without her sister's support of her education, her parents would expect her to work a full-time job and concentrate on helping financially support the family.

Jackie's older siblings also helped her pursue a bachelor's degree. She credited her older sister moving back home and contributing to the family's expenses with being able to transfer to Metro U. If her sister did not take over Jackie's financial contribution to rent and household bills, she would have had to continue to work on a full-time basis and possibly only enroll part-time at a four-year institution. She also would not have completed her degree in two years at Metro U. Jackie recognized that she would not have earned her parents' emotional and financial support without the initial backing of her older brothers and sister who encouraged her to continue her education. Coupled with her boyfriend's financial and emotional support of her academic goals, Jackie finished her bachelor's degree at the end of the 2009–2010 school year as planned. The bonding social capital resources that she accessed kept her continually enrolled in college.

Older siblings were instrumental in the success of some of the Metro U. students profiled in this study. They often sacrificed their own secondary or postsecondary education to help with the family's living expenses. Julia's brother attended community college as a part-time student so that he could help support the family. This arrangement allowed Julia to attend Metro U. on a full-time basis. Alba's sister withdrew early from high school so that she could work full-time and help with household bills. Jackie's three older siblings either withdrew early from high school or ceased their education after high school in large part to assist their parents with family expenses. All of these examples demonstrate that older siblings often sacrificed their own academic goals for the betterment of their younger siblings.

Friends and peers

Students' friends and peers were also instrumental in their success as college students. Friends and peers supported students both at the secondary and postsecondary levels throughout college preparation and matriculation. They also provided much-needed sources of bonding and bridging social capital to undocumented Metro U. students. Recall that Monica, Julia, Alba, Alejandra, and Manny all drew support from high school peers and acquaintances when planning for their eventual college enrollment. Monica, Alba, and Alejandra received individual support from their close documented and undocumented friends. Their friends encouraged them to pursue their college dreams while in high school. They also benefitted from information and contacts their friends assembled regarding undocumented-friendly scholarships and academic opportunities. These friends continued to support them as they pursued their academic careers at Metro U. Knowing that their friends believed in their ability to earn a bachelor's degree was encouraging when they encountered repeated financial and academic obstacles.

Julia and Manny also benefitted from formal high school support groups for undocumented students. Both helped establish and lead student-initiated groups on their respective high school campuses. These groups provided Julia and Manny with a significantly larger peer group that helped them broaden their social contacts and resources. Group members regularly coordinated information events and campus fundraisers for undocumented student scholarships. The groups also collaborated with undocumented student college support groups on local college campuses. Julia and Manny received encouragement and resources from current undocumented college students that helped them prepare for their own postsecondary education. These college students also helped Julia and Manny strategize how to overcome anticipated and unexpected difficulties while attending Metro U. Both students believed that positive experiences in their high school support groups helped them overcome the initial stress they encountered when transitioning to college.

The Metro U. students in this study also received important financial and emotional support from their college peers and friends. As I elaborate later in this chapter, all of the students cited their participation in IMAGINE as important to their success at Metro U. They received constant encouragement from IMAGINE members who intimately knew the realities of being an undocumented college student. Students regularly exchanged information about campus academic resources and employment opportunities that they depended on in order to continue their education. Julia used fellow IMAGINE members' strategies to enroll in overenrolled and closed courses. Stephanie and Jackie became IMAGINE student leaders so as to increase the visibility of the group on campus and network on behalf of a largely invisible campus minority. Most importantly, the study participants found the constant comfort, assistance, and inspiration of their fellow undocumented college students invaluable to their matriculation. Friends and student peers helped Metro U. undocumented students stay positive throughout the college application and matriculation processes.

As with the previous finding, supportive relatives and friends ultimately benefitting the students' educational trajectories is not an uncommon finding in educational studies. What makes this finding unique is that undocumented students' families are usually more dependent on students' contributions—especially financial supplements—for sustaining the entire family's living arrangements. Supplementing an undocumented student's living and/or educational expenses often strains the family's financial situation; the majority of undocumented students' families cannot manage the expenses incurred by a student enrolling at a four-year institution. Even students like Cristina whose parents could afford to pay all of her academic and non-academic expenses experienced a financial burden that required her mother to start working outside of the home for extra money. Lending financial or emotional support to an undocumented college student who has limited opportunities to obtain a better-paying job in the future is difficult for many students' families to endorse.

Family- and peer-based social capital proved integral to Metro U. students' matriculation. The expectations of college attendance as well as the resources found inside and outside of these close social networks enabled students to overcome the hurdles they experienced while matriculating. All of the profiled Metro U. students relied on the consistent financial, academic, and personal resources furnished by relatives and friends. The third finding focuses on how students' beliefs about their immigration status affected their social capital resources and matriculation.

Finding 3: Perceptions about Immigration Status Affected Students' Matriculation and Social Capital Development
The nine profiled Metro U. students regularly reflected on how their immigration status affected their matriculation. As I describe in my responses to questions 3 and 4, students' perceptions about their status directly influenced their college-going experiences including how they developed and accessed bridging and bonding social capital. Beliefs about one's immigration status were not static. Rather students referenced their present and future statuses when discussing their impact on their college experiences. Metro U. students explained that at times their immigration status had been an obstacle to overcome while at other times it had been a gift that made them more resilient to academic difficulties. While Metro U. undocumented students overwhelmingly saw themselves as ordinary college students, they did acknowledge that their immigration statuses affected why and how they pursued a college education.

Documenting why students' immigration statuses contributed to their success was complicated since all of the nine profiled students each had their own personal immigration situation. Recall that Julia and Jackie had pending relative-sponsored immigration applications that they hoped would alter their status in the coming years. Cristina, Stephanie, Jackie, and Manny did not have outstanding immigration applications but came from mixed immigration status families in which select relatives were U.S. residents or citizens. Monica, Alba, and Luz had no U.S.-resident or -citizen relatives. Each of the nine students had varying levels of knowledge about their individual immigration status including relevant immigration laws and procedures. Students also discovered their status at different times during their academic careers. The only constant in all of these undocumented immigrants' lives was that they were all Metro U. undergraduates earning bachelor's degrees. There were several ways in which immigration status significantly affected students' educational trajectories, including their acquisition of valuable social capital—when students discovered their status, projections about their future immigration status, and beliefs about one's roles and responsibilities as an undocumented immigrant.

<u>Timing of notification</u>
Each student in this study discovered his or her immigration status at different times during primary or secondary school. The timing of their

discovery directly impacted their ability to procure relevant social capital resources and pursue a postsecondary education. Only three people in the study—Cristina, Jackie, and Manny—were unaware of their immigration status until high school. Cristina and Manny discovered their statuses in 11th grade while Jackie found out during 12th grade. Discovering that they were undocumented affected each student differently.

Recall that Cristina was shocked by the news of her "new identity" as an undocumented immigrant. While grappling with a new identity had been difficult for Cristina, she was grateful for her parents' delay in telling her the truth about her status. She believed that because her parents waited until high school to inform her, she did not have the opportunity to question her parents' and school's expectations for her to attend college. Thus, she took advantage of the bonding social capital in her home and high school environments that set the expectation of college attendance. She also did not have the opportunity to become despondent or doubt whether she belonged on a university campus. Cristina's decision to not inform any of her secondary instructors or counselors that she was undocumented left her foreclosed from any undocumented-related college-going information such institutional agents may have held. She was left with no bridging social capital resources or contacts that helped her transition to community college.

Jackie and Manny were less surprised by the news that they were undocumented. Jackie recalled that her family's economic struggles made more sense once she realized that they had been constrained by their immigration status. By the time Jackie found out about her status, her only option was to enroll in a local community college and pay her own academic fees with personal earnings. Nevertheless she believed that because she did not know the truth until later in high school, she participated in the AVID Program and prepared for college admission. Like Cristina, Jackie took advantage of the bonding social capital available among AVID students and staff members. Remember Jackie's surprise as she experienced a college-going environment for the first time. "My family had no expectations for me to go to college. I am the first to go …. AVID was crazy because everyone was going to go to college." Jackie's relationships with her AVID advisor and classmates also served as bridging social capital that exposed her to new resources related to attending college. The information and resources that she accessed while in AVID allowed her to acquire practical, albeit general college-going social capital that would have been unavailable to her outside of the program.

As the oldest of five children, Manny knew that he was born in Mexico but never suspected that he was undocumented. Similar to Cristina and Monica, he was pleased that his parents delayed disclosing his immigration status. Once he discovered his status, he immediately began consulting with his teachers and counselors about his predicament. They encouraged him to identify sources of bridging social capital that would enable him to attend college. He applied to undocumented-friendly scholarships and networked with older undocumented students who were applying to college. Similar to Cristina and Monica, Manny feared that he might not have prepared to attend college if he had known his immigration status earlier in his educational career. Instead he modified his preparation for college by accessing relevant social capital held by various members of his high school community.

The remaining Metro U. students were aware of their immigration status earlier than Cristina, Jackie, and Manny. Prior knowledge of their immigration status—even if incomplete—allowed these Metro U. students to prepare for college. For example, Monica, Julia, Luz, and Alejandra each approached their postsecondary education from the perspective of an informed undocumented immigrant; they accepted the challenge of attending college without access to financial aid and traditional student employment opportunities. All four shared their immigration status with secondary instructors and counselors. They devised practical, comprehensive college plans while still in high school that facilitated their shared goal of enrolling at a four-year institution. Having a more comprehensive understanding of their status and its implications while still in high school ultimately benefitted these women when pursuing their college goals. They were able to take advantage of various bridging and bonding social capital resources while still enrolled in high school. They established relationships and accessed resources that would be of use to them throughout their postsecondary studies.

Not all of the students who were aware of their immigration status were able to start planning their college careers as undocumented immigrants early on in high school. Stephanie benefitted from knowing her status early on in life. She excelled in her studies and extracurricular activities during primary and secondary school so that she would be a competitive college applicant. Even though she did not have access to knowledgeable instructors and counselors with relevant sources of bridging social capital while in high school, she did benefit from her parents' expectations that she attend college regardless of her immigration status. Her well-developed bonding social capital with her parents was crucial in her decision to enroll at a local community college; her parents would not allow her to defer or reject her lifelong plan to complete a college degree. In retrospect, Stephanie was grateful that she discovered the limitations of her status during 12th grade. She feared that the depression she experienced during her senior year would have been more destructive if she had found out earlier in high school.

Future immigration status

The students in this study gauged their overall ability to complete a college degree not only on their present immigration status but also their future status. Monica, Stephanie, and Alejandra all received freshman admission offers to attend prestigious public and private institutions. While the attraction of attending a more selective institution was alluring, all three women chose less-expensive options. They either enrolled at a community college or at Metro U. because of the more affordable academic fees and vicinity to their homes. They anticipated having to pay for their entire education without the help of federal and state financial aid. All three believed that the chances of the DREAM Act or comprehensive immigration reform passing during their college-going years were slight. Thus, they planned their college careers using the bridging and bonding social capital resources they perceived available to them—mostly through institutional agents, relatives, friends, and community members—as undocumented immigrants.

Cristina and Luz, eligible to apply to the UC as freshmen, only applied to less-expensive four-year institutions like Metro U. close to their homes. They reasoned that applying to institutions where they could not afford to attend was impractical; they had a better chance of using the financial resources within their families and existing social relationships to complete their degrees. Even Julia and Jackie who had pending immigration applications did not consider more expensive public and private postsecondary options outside of their immediate area. Like Monica, Stephanie, and Alejandra, Julia and Jackie could not justify taking the chance of enrolling at institutions that were more expensive or located far from home based on projections of future financial aid eligibility or access to undocumented-friendly scholarships and employment opportunities.

Projections about future immigration status also affected students' postsecondary plans and matriculation. All of the students hoped that they would be able to change their status in the future by a relative-sponsored application, immigration reform, or in a couple of cases, marriage. Monica believed that because she was undocumented, she had been particularly motivated to attend college and seek the resources needed to realize her dream.

> I came [to Metro U.] and I was like, "I am not going to tell anyone about my status. I was like, what's the point?" When I started to get involved [on campus and in the community] and see all of these kids get involved with these other non-profits and being activists, it empowered me to be less afraid to say, "I am here, I am undocumented, I am Latina."

Coupled with the possibility of changing her immigration status is the future via federal legislation, Monica chose to pursue a postsecondary degree with the help of her family, instructors, counselors, and peers. She believed that it was a sound investment in her future as a documented immigrant without employment, political, and social restrictions.

Other students like Alba did not focus on their immigration status as an impossible obstacle. Instead, she used her struggle to attain a college education as preparation for overcoming future hurdles. Because she believed that she eventually would be able to change her status as a result of immigration reform, she decided to be open about her immigration status and access any and all social capital that could benefit her matriculation. Alejandra saw a future as a professional social worker working with members of her community. She, too, was less focused on being an undocumented immigrant who faced constant impediments while trying to pursue her education. She concentrated on her future career and involvement in her community as a former undocumented immigrant who overcame structural obstacles like racism and classism to achieve her goals. Alejandra did not hesitate in asking for help from institutional agents, friends, and relatives. She actively sought new sources of social capital that she could use in financing her Metro U. education.

All of the students in this study chose to attend Metro U. because they believed that they could successfully earn a bachelor's degree from the institution as undocumented immigrants. Students were more confident that they could access assistance and resources within existing social circles over the years to acquire their degrees. Further, the university was a practical, sensible option in terms of costs and location for enrollment compared to other institutions. Their families as well as their respective secondary and postsecondary institutional agents endorsed their decisions to attend Metro U. considering students' current and future immigration-related limitations. Metro U. offered established academic, financial, and human resources and social capital networks for undocumented matriculants.

Roles and responsibilities

Immigration status also affected the students' perceived roles and responsibilities. As I elaborate later in this chapter, many of the students believed that as undocumented immigrants, they were responsible for disproving negative stereotypes about their community. Stephanie regularly shared her status with fellow students so as to educate others about undocumented students on campus and in the community. She felt that she could demonstrate to other undocumented students that earning a bachelor's degree was possible without the support of traditional financial aid. Alejandra also believed that as an undocumented student, she had particular responsibilities to her community. She thought that she could more effectively help *la raza* by being a college-educated professional. Monica had recently appropriated the term "undocumented" and proudly identified as an undocumented immigrant, woman, and student. She explained that by appropriating the word, she had a responsibility to bring dignity to the term by overcoming the obstacles she met while pursuing a higher education.

Some students felt that it was their duty to pursue a college education so as to inspire relatives to do the same. They reasoned that if they were able to complete a degree while undocumented, documented and U.S.-citizen relatives and friends would be less inclined to forego postsecondary enrollment. Further, many believed that it was because of their relatives' focus on education and the strong bonding social capital that they experienced in secondary school that they committed to attend college regardless of the obstacles. Recall that Luz believed that by completing a bachelor's degree, her younger sister, who is also undocumented, would be more likely to enroll in college. Jackie felt that being a first-generation college student would inspire her U.S.-born sister and nieces to pursue a college education. "I feel like I have to set an example for all of the kids. My parents expect me to do that, too, since I didn't have kids or get married young. My example shows them another way of life." Manny also wanted to be a positive example for his younger siblings.

Beliefs about one's immigration status shaped students' matriculation and respective social capital development. All of the nine profiled Metro U. students explicitly or implicitly tied their own participation in postsecondary education to their current immigration status as well as their prospects of changing their status in the future. They shared their current immigration status with others in order to procure existing and build future sources of social capital beneficial to their matriculation. Students viewed their matriculation as a responsibility to both maintain and expand the available bridging and bonding social capital resources for current and prospective undocumented college students. Sharing social capital resources strengthened students' ties with one another and ensured the passing of resources to others. Further, students saw their own college completion affecting relatives' and friends'—both documented and undocumented—chances of completing a postsecondary degree. Metro U. students were in a position to promote an alternative and positive image of undocumented immigrants.

Undocumented college students pursue a postsecondary education for personal, political, and social reasons. These otherwise ordinary college students exhibit an exceptional devotion to their academic goals. They do not shy away from the challenges that they face as undocumented immigrants. They are exceptional by way of their determination in pursuing an unguaranteed college education amidst uncertain future job prospects. Why certain individuals are successful is a product of individual circumstances, the social capital they can access during college preparation and matriculation, and how they view their immigration status. The nine profiled Metro U. students received support and assistance from select institutional agents, relatives, and friends. They accessed both bridging and bonding social capital that gave them the resources and know-how to counter the obstacles they faced as undocumented immigrants. I now turn to a discussion of the four research questions that guided this study.

Answering the Questions

The majority of undocumented college students pursue a postsecondary education with extensive reflection, consideration, and planning. As they begin to consider pursuing a college degree, they evaluate their circumstances, organize their resources, and plan for future obstacles. The purpose of this study was to describe the ways undocumented immigrants successfully pursue a postsecondary degree at a four-year institution. Each of the study's four questions helps explain how undocumented students go about matriculation.

Question 1: How do undocumented college students develop, maintain, and exchange social capital?

Metro U. students depended on various sources of social capital to successfully prepare for and enroll in college. Chapter 4 documents each student's journey to college including how relatives, friends, and institutional agents were instrumental in providing students with relevant information about how to attend college as undocumented immigrants. The students developed, maintained, and exchanged social capital in myriad ways and settings. Students regularly shared pertinent information regarding AB 540, undocumented student scholarships, employment opportunities, and community and political service positions with each other at the secondary and postsecondary levels. Some students received information from their undocumented peers via high school and college student support groups, such as Metro U.'s IMAGINE group. Others discovered information from their undocumented and documented classmates and relatives. Most of the Metro U. students also received vital undocumented student information and resources through secondary and postsecondary institutional agents who supported them during the college application and matriculation processes. These exchanges of social capital highlight the influence and importance of institutional-, family-, and peer-based networks in assisting undocumented students with their educational goals.

The information and resources students accessed made the difference in their ability to pursue a college education. Building and exchanging social capital entailed regularly sharing relevant and timely information and resources with other students and institutional agents for further distribution. Students who identified as being undocumented immigrants to peers and key institutional agents were often given access to unknown resources and information that benefitted their educational plans. Undocumented students maintaining and exchanging social capital depended on continued access to community nonprofit organizations, supportive faculty and staff members, and fellow student allies who supported undocumented immigrants' right to a postsecondary education.

Question 2: Do the social support networks of undocumented college students factor into educational outcomes?

All of the Metro U. students benefitted academically from informal and formal social support networks at their respective high schools and community colleges as well as Metro U. Students successfully pursued their college degrees with the financial and moral support of others. They depended on relatives for financial support to help pay academic expenses and emotional support to help push them toward their academic goals. They relied on friends and institutional agents for important college admissions and matriculation information. Students put faith in community organizations to represent their interests in the local and national immigration debates. Metro U. students relied on others to fill in the gaps left by an educational system that did not directly acknowledge or serve their unique needs.

The social networks of undocumented college students were varied. Each network fulfilled different needs for different students. For instance, the IMAGINE group provided some students with moral support and bonding social capital available from peers. For others, it provided bridging social capital resources to learn about employment and academic opportunities. Nevertheless, IMAGINE was viewed by all of the study participants as a communal organization though which the students reliably accessed different types of pertinent bonding and bridging social capital. IMAGINE was unique in that undocumented students could learn about undocumented-related issues from experienced and knowledgeable peers and institutional agents sympathetic to their cause.

Question 3: How do experiences of exclusion shape the educational identity and consciousness of undocumented students?
Political, societal, legal, and academic exclusion affected all nine Metro U. students at some point during their college preparation and matriculation. Foreclosed from traditional financial aid options, students pursued a college degree without the support of the state or federal government. They encountered limited employment options as they sought work primarily in the underground economy or at community nonprofit organizations. Students also pursued an education while national and state politicians debated the merits of immigration reform and educational benefits for undocumented immigrants.

Given these experiences and realities, the students in this study overwhelmingly believed that the exclusion they faced as a result of their immigration status positively influenced their academic goals. Even if initially deterred from enrolling in college, students were more determined to complete their degrees regardless of familial and personal sacrifices. The Metro U. students struggled to raise the money to attend college and were more willing to compromise on where they attended because they were undocumented. Students adjusted their expectations of their educational timelines and their future employment prospects. They regularly strategized and sought help from campus and community allies when they were told that they could not attend college. They procured the social capital resources that aided them in their matriculation available both inside and outside of their communities. Students turned to political activism on and off campus in order to help make their personal and other undocumented students' academic goals materialize. They supported state and national efforts to expand academic opportunities to undocumented immigrants. Metro U. students created a positive college experience and identity for themselves by uniting with other undocumented students and allies in seeking expanded personal and communal academic opportunities.

Question 4: How do the contours of an undocumented student's identity enable or disable academic performance?
The students in this study did not all agree with what it meant to be an undocumented immigrant. Each student had a particular way of viewing their individual and group identities, especially in contrast to documented immigrants and U.S. citizens. Some students believed that being undocumented did not influence their perceptions of what was possible in terms of their educational attainment and future job prospects. These students overwhelmingly felt that American society did not treat them in a negative way. Rather, they saw the US as providing economic and educational opportunities absent in their birth countries. Other students believed that they were systematically discriminated against because of their undocumented status. The constant social, economic, and educational discrimination they encountered shaped their identities as undocumented immigrant college students. There was no consensus about what it meant to be an undocumented immigrant pursuing a postsecondary education.

Even though the students profiled in this study had different ideas about their undocumented identity, they all largely benefitted academically from being undocumented immigrants. They appropriated many of the values they witnessed in their families—namely hard work and determination—and applied them to pursuing their academic goals. Recall that all of the nine students profiled in this study respected their parents' decisions to immigrate to the US for better economic and educational opportunities. Students viewed their undocumented statuses and their families' subsequent sacrifices as a quasi mandate to pursue a college education; they must complete a college degree so that their families' lifelong dreams could be fulfilled.

Students also drew upon American society's more negative opinions of undocumented immigrants as motivation to pursue their educational goals. Some students set out to disprove society's expectations that undocumented immigrants were largely uneducated and unmotivated. Students also discussed how they wanted to disprove members of the Latino community that summarized their presence in the US as mere lawbreakers. Belonging to a minority within a minority—that is being a college student within the undocumented immigrant community—was an accomplishment many Metro U. students felt would help shape the national immigration reform debate. Being an undocumented college student was proof for some study participants that their primary and secondary education guaranteed by *Plyler v. Doe* (1982) was a sound investment for the larger national community. Metro U. undocumented students relied on their own positive interpretation of their undocumented immigrant identity to drive their postsecondary goals.

These nine Metro U. students actively pursued their educational goals largely due to the fact that they had a social support system to rely on if and when they encountered problems. They had the opportunity to troubleshoot financial, academic, and personal conflicts with fellow undocumented students and supporters. The promise that an individual—whether a student peer, counselor, instructor, or relative within a bridging or bonding social support network—would be there to help undocumented students overcome obstacles was vital to their success at Metro U. I will now discuss this study's implications for future research before offering some concluding thoughts.

RESEARCH IMPLICATIONS
This study was small in scope—it focused on the experiences of nine undocumented students attending Metro U. Sixteen additional interviews with other undocumented Metro U. students as well as 15 interviews with UC and CSU students supplemented the primary interviews and observations. The study was meant to focus on the actions and experiences of those students attending a public comprehensive HSI in a metropolitan area with a large and established undocumented immigrant population. The findings are not wholly applicable to other undocumented students attending dissimilar institutions in other areas of the state or country. The larger community surrounding Metro U. as well as the campus's unique political and social climate influenced the experiences of the nine profiled students. All of the students reported relatively positive educational experiences at Metro U. and their respective high schools. They easily blended in both on and off campus. Study respondents were not singled out as undocumented immigrants by way of their physical appearance. Rather,

all of the study participants chose to self identify as undocumented immigrants.

Given the unique nature of the Metro U. environment and context, research on this small and unknown population would benefit greatly from more gender, ethnic, and geographic diversity. This study was both female- and Latino-centric since the majority of participants were Latinas. Educational researchers and practitioners would yield a more comprehensive view of undocumented immigrant college students from knowing more about how male and non-Latino undocumented immigrants pursue a postsecondary education. Researchers would also benefit from knowing how individuals from non-metropolitan areas in states without undocumented-friendly in-state academic fee policies prepare for matriculation. For example, research focusing on male Asian immigrants studying at institutions located outside of large traditional immigrant-receiving areas would be a logical next step in studying undocumented immigrant college students. This study, with its limited socioeconomic diversity, points to different educational trajectories for those students hailing from more affluent and educated backgrounds. It is reasonable to assume that non-Latino and Latino immigrants growing up in suburban and rural areas have different educational experiences at the postsecondary level.

Another research implication of this study is the need to gain broader access to the undocumented college student population. As mentioned earlier in this book, statewide accounting of undocumented college students is incomplete and possibly inaccurate. A more thorough accounting of undocumented immigrant students enrolled in postsecondary education would potentially allow researchers to conduct quantitative studies on larger samples of students. Identifying student participants for this study was arduous and time-consuming. Further, building relationships within the undocumented student community was not limited to the year of data collection but required networking with contacts and students in previous years. More quality qualitative research could be conducted on the group if researchers had an easier time identifying students with the help of campus administrators.

Changing the theoretical lens by which researchers examine undocumented immigrants' postsecondary experiences may also yield informative results. This study employed a social capital theoretical framework in order to better understand students' college preparation and matriculation amidst personal, institutional, and societal challenges. Employing resiliency theory could provide more insight into how individual students are able to overcome adversities, challenges, and stressors to achieve successful adaptation to their circumstances. This theory and others could afford educators with more evidence about why particular students succeed in completing a college education given little if no traditional institutional and governmental support.

Finally, the need for research on this group of students is vital to the continuing national conversation on immigration reform. As of this writing, the United States Congress is considering comprehensive immigration reform. Documenting the educational trajectories of students at Metro U. and other institutions contributes to the diversity and accuracy of information lawmakers and policymakers can access when making decisions. Acknowledging these students' academic and personal accomplishments promotes an immigration reform discussion that is inclusive, complex, and multidimensional.

CONCLUSIONS
The purpose of this study was to describe how a group of undocumented college students successfully matriculated at a four-year institution. The intention was to provide the reader with an idea of how several undocumented immigrants accessed their familial, academic, and financial resources and social capital to pursue a postsecondary education without guaranteed access to a college education. Following these nine Metro U. students during the 2009–2010 academic year, I discussed why and how students overcame significant obstacles and setbacks in accomplishing their educational goals. I also chronicled how students utilized their undocumented identity as a source of inspiration and motivation to continue going to school. I described how being an undocumented college student was not so much a solitary experience but a communal experience for students. Students relied on their relatives, friends, educators, and undocumented peers to find their way successfully through college.

Cristina, Monica, Julia, Stephanie, Alba, Luz, Alejandra, Jackie, and Manny are ordinary Metro U. students. Their academic success is testament to their hard work and determination and that of their families. They live their lives within a society that does not guarantee their access to a postsecondary education. They prepare to live as informed and educated individuals in a future society that legally recognizes their presence, talents, and contributions.

Appendix A

STUDENT RECRUITMENT FLYER
Are you currently an undergraduate student? Would you like to see more students like you pursue a higher education?
If you answered "yes" to either of these questions, you might be interested in participating in a research study. Your participation is voluntary; you must be aged 18 or older to participate.

Research Study
My name is Lisa D. Garcia and I am a graduate student and researcher at the University of Southern California. I would like to invite you to participate in a research study that I will be conducting academic year 2009–2010. The study will look at the issues that undocumented students deal with during the entire college-going process. I am meeting with students from your institution who have expressed that they are undocumented and are currently pursuing a postsecondary degree. I am interested in talking to this group of students because there is very little public information about the experiences of undocumented students as they attend college, graduate, and transition into the working world.

If you agree to participate in this study, you and I will meet at least one time during this current academic year. When we meet, I will ask you questions about how you prepared for college as well as your actual college-going experience. I will also ask you about your opportunities to pursue a higher education. I will ask you permission to audio record the interview. However, audio recording the interview is not compulsory for participation in the study and you may choose not to be audio recorded. Although the information you provide to the researcher may be made public, your identity will remain anonymous. Your name, address, or other identifiable information, such as your student ID number, will not be collected or associated with your response.

If you think you might be interested in participating in the study, please review the attached consent form for more details. Should you have any questions or concerns, or are interested in participating, please feel free to contact me.

Appendix B

STUDY INFORMATION SHEET
University of Southern California
Rossier School of Education
Information Sheet for Non-Medical Research
Consent to Participate in Research
"Undocumented College Students"

Individual Student Interview
You are invited to participate in a research study conducted by Lisa D. Garcia and William G. Tierney, Ph.D. (faculty advisor), from the University of Southern California. The research is being conducted in order to fulfill the requirements of a degree. You are eligible to participate because you are an undocumented student currently attending a four-year postsecondary institution. You must be at least 18 years of age to participate. Your participation is voluntary. You should read the information below, and ask questions about anything you do not understand, before deciding whether or not to participate. Please take as much time as you need to read the consent form. You may also decide to discuss it with your family or friends. You will be given a copy of this form.

Purpose of the Study
The researchers are interested in finding out how undocumented students navigate the college-going process. Particular attention will be paid to the impact of one's undocumented status, college preparatory programs, California Assembly Bill 540 (AB 540), private and/or merit-based financial aid programs, and family/peer/community support on college-going rates of this population.

Procedures
If you volunteer to participate in this study, we would ask you to participate in a 60–90 minute individual interview. We would also ask you to participate in informal observations during undocumented student club meetings and activities.

Interviews will be scheduled at a time convenient to you and the researcher, in an office at USC or a location of your choosing. Questions include: "Describe your experiences in the U.S. educational system" and "Tell me about how American society treats undocumented immigrants." They may also include the discussion of your plans for the duration of your college career and post-college study or employment plans.

The interview will be audio-taped with your permission. If you do not want to be audio-taped you can continue with your participation; handwritten notes will be taken.

Potential Risks and Discomforts
You may feel uncomfortable or unsure about discussing your college experience and your plans for employment or your immigration status. You may also feel uneasy about being audio taped. You are not required to answer any questions that you don't want to.

Potential Benefits to Subjects and/or Society
You will not directly benefit from participating in this study. The information you provide during interviews may lead to a greater understanding of the experiences of undocumented students who are preparing to attend college or who have graduated.

It is hoped this research will help inform educational policies that directly affect undocumented students in postsecondary education.

Payment/Compensation for Participation
There is no payment or compensation for your participation in this study. You will not be reimbursed for any costs incurred as a result of your participation. For example, parking or transportation costs will not be reimbursed by the researchers.

Confidentiality
There will be no information recorded in connection with this study and that can be identified with you. Your name, address, or other

information that may identify you will not be collected during this research study.

Only members of the research team will have access to the data associated with this study. The data will be stored on a password-protected computer owned by the principal investigator. Your professors, college administrators, or other institutional personnel will not have access to your responses.

The interview will be transcribed by Lisa D. Garcia, Principal Investigator. Only the researchers will have access to the audio files, which will be stored on a password-protected computer.

The data will be stored for three years after the study has been completed and then destroyed.

When the results of the research are published or discussed in conferences, no information will be included that would reveal your identity.

Participation and Withdrawal

Your participation is voluntary. Your refusal to participate will involve no penalty or loss of benefits to which you are otherwise entitled. You may withdraw your consent at any time and discontinue participation without penalty. You are not waiving any legal claims, rights or remedies because of your participation in this research study. The investigator may withdraw you from this research if circumstances arise which warrant doing so.

Alternatives to Participation

Your alternative is to not participate. Your grades will not be affected whether or not you participate in the research study.

Rights of Research Subjects

If you have any questions about your rights as a study subject or you would like to speak with someone independent of the research team to have questions answered about the research, or in the event the research staff cannot be reached, please contact the University Park IRB, Office of the Vice Provost for Research Advancement, Stonier Hall, Room 224A, Los Angeles, CA 90089-1146, 213.821.5272 or upirb@usc.edu, or the Metropolitan University IRB.

Identification of Investigators

If you have any questions or concerns about the research, please feel free to contact Lisa D. Garcia or William G. Tierney at 213.740.7218 during regular office hours—8:30 a.m. to 5:00 p.m., Monday through Friday.

Signature of Research Participant (Optional)

By signing this consent form you indicate that you have read the form and agree voluntarily to participate in the study. If you choose not to take part there will be no penalty or loss of benefits to which you are entitled. If you agree to take part, you are free to withdraw from it at any time. Likewise, no penalty or loss of benefits to which you are otherwise entitled will occur.

I agree to participate in the study, Undocumented College Students, as set out above.

_____   _____

Signature   **Date**

THIS PROJECT HAS BEEN REVIEWED ˙ BY THE METROPOLITAN UNIVERSITY INSTITUTIONAL REVIEW BOARD FOR THE PROTECTION OF HUMAN SUBJECTS IN RESEARCH. ADDITIONAL CONCERNS, COMPLAINTS, OR QUESTIONS REGARDING YOUR RIGHTS AS A RESEARCH PARTICIPANT SHOULD BE DIRECTED TO THE DIRECTOR OF RESEARCH AND DEVELOPMENT.

Appendix C

PROTOCOL FOR STUDENT INTERVIEWS
Background Questions
1. Describe when you arrived in the US.
2. Describe your family background in terms of educational attainment and socioeconomic standing.
3. Describe where you grew up including neighborhoods and living situations.
4. What is your current immigration status?
   a. Do you have a pending immigration case?
   b. Do you anticipate changing your status in the near future?

Educational Background
5. Describe your experiences in the U.S. educational system.
6. Tell me about your family's educational expectations.
7. Tell me about your personal educational expectations.

College Going and Social Capital
8. What experiences made you begin thinking about going to college?
9. How did you prepare as an undocumented student to go to college?
   a. Who helped you prepare and apply for college?
   b. Did student peers help you navigate the college application process?
10. How has being undocumented influenced the decisions that you have made in relation to your higher education?
11. How did you apply to college? Community college or four-year college first?

12. Why did you choose to attend your college?
13. Tell me about how you finance college?
14. Tell me about how college is going for you.
    a. Who helps you continue your education?
    b. What role does your family and friends have in you attending college?
    c. What role do fellow undocumented students have in you attending college?
15. Tell me about AB 540.
    a. How did you find out about the law?
    b. Do you qualify for the reduced fees?
    c. How has AB 540 affected your higher education?
16. Tell me about the DREAM Act.

Feelings of Inclusion/Exclusion
17. Tell me about how American society treats undocumented immigrants.
18. How have experiences of exclusion (as an undocumented student) shaped your educational identity and consciousness?
19. Explain how you identify as an undocumented immigrant.

References

Abrego, L. J. (2006). "I can't go to college because I don't have papers": Incorporation patterns of Latino undocumented youth. *Latino Studies, 4,* 212–231.

Abrego, L. J. (2008). Legitimacy, social identity, and the mobilization of law: The effects of Assembly Bill 540 on undocumented students in California. *Law & Society, 33,* 709–734.

Adelman, C. (1996, October 4). The truth about remedial work (Point of view). *The Chronicle of Higher Education,* p. A56.

Adelman, C. (1998). The kiss of death? An alternative view of college remediation. *National Crosstalk, 6*(3), 11.

Adelman, C. (2006). *The toolbox revisited: Paths to degree completion from high school through college.* Washington, DC: U.S. Department of Education.

Adler, P. A., & Adler, P. (1994). Observational techniques. In N. K. Denzin & Y. S. Lincoln (Eds.), *Handbook of qualitative research* (pp. 377–392). Thousand Oaks, CA: Sage.

Adler, P. S., & Kwon, S. (2002). Prospects for a new concept. *The Academy of Management Review, 27,* 17–40.

Allen, W., & Solorzano, D. (2001). Affirmative action, educational equity and campus racial climate: A case study of the University of Michigan Law School. *La Raza Law Journal, 12,* 237–363.

Angrosino, M. V., & Mays de Perez, K. A. (2000). Rethinking observation: From method to context. In N. K. Denzin & Y. S. Lincoln (Eds.), *Handbook of qualitative research* (2nd ed., pp. 673–702). Thousand Oaks, CA: Sage.

Atkinson, P., & Hammersley, M. (1994). Ethnography and participant observation. In N. K. Denzin & Y. S. Lincoln (Eds.), *Handbook of qualitative research* (pp. 248–261). Thousand Oaks, CA: Sage.

Bailey, T. R., & Weininger, E. B. (2002). Performance, graduation, and transfer of immigrants and natives in City University of New York Community Colleges. *Educational Evaluation and Policy Analysis, 24*, 359–377.

Batalova, J., & Fix, M. (2006). *Immigration backgrounder: New estimates of unauthorized youth eligible for legal status under the DREAM Act.* Washington, DC: The Migration Policy Institute.

Becker, G. S. (1993). *Human capital: A theoretical and empirical analysis, with special reference to education* (3rd ed.) Chicago, IL: University of Chicago Press.

Blackburn, J. C. (2009, June). *Reporting new and continuing students receiving the benefits of AB 540.* Retrieved from www.calstate.edu/acadAff/codedmemos/AA-2009-12.pdf

Blackwell, J. (1981). *Mainstreaming outsiders: The production of Black professionals.* Bayside, NY: General Hall.

Boeije, H. (2002). A purposeful approach to the constant comparative method in the analysis of qualitative interviews. *Quantity and Quality, 36*, 391–409.

Bogdan, R. C., & Biklen, S. K. (1992). *Qualitative research for education: An introduction to theory and methods.* Boston, MA: Ally & Bacon.

Bogdan, R. C., & Taylor, S. J. (1975). *Introduction to qualitative research methods: A phenomenological approach to the social sciences.* New York, NY: John Wiley & Sons.

Bourdieu, P. (1986). The forms of capital. In J. G. Richardson (Ed.), *Handbook of theory and research for the sociology of education* (pp. 241–258). New York, NY: Greenwood Press.

Brubaker, R. (1985). Rethinking classical theory: The sociological vision of Pierre Bourdieu. *Theory and Society, 14*, 745–775.

Casas-Frier, & Hansen, R. (2006). *Immigrant students: Gaining visibility.* Sacramento, CA: Faculty Association of California Community Colleges.

Chavez, L. R. (1998). *Shadowed lives: Undocumented immigrants in American society* (2nd ed.). Fort Worth, TX: Harcourt Brace College.

Coleman, J. S. (1988). Social capital in the creation of human capital. *The American Journal of Sociology, 94*(Suppl.), S95–S120.

Coleman, J. S. (1990). *Foundations of social theory*. Cambridge, MA: Harvard University Press.

Contreras, F. (2009). Sin papeles y rompiendo barreras: Latino students and the challenges of persisting in college. *Harvard Educational Review, 79*(4), 610–631.

Conway, K. M. (2009). Exploring persistence of immigrant and native students in an urban community college. *The Review of Higher Education, 32*, 321–352.

Creswell, J. W. (2007). *Qualitative inquiry & research design: Choosing among five approaches* (2nd ed.). Thousand Oaks, CA: Sage.

De Genova, N. P. (2002). Migrant "illegality" and deportability in everyday life. *Annual Review of Anthropology, 31*, 419–447.

De Genova, N. P. (2004). The legal production of Mexican/migrant "illegality." *Latino Studies, 2*, 160–185.

Dennis, J. M., Phinney, J. S., & Chuateco, L. I. (2005). The role of motivation, parental support, and peer support in the academic success of ethnic minority first-generation college students. *Journal of College Student Development, 46*, 223–236.

Denzin, N. K., & Lincoln, Y. S. (2000). The discipline and practice of qualitative research. In N. K. Denzin & Y. S. Lincoln (Eds.), *Handbook of qualitative research* (2nd ed., pp. 1–25). Thousand Oaks, CA: Sage.

Dika, S. L., & Singh, K. (2002). Applications of social capital in educational literature: A critical synthesis. *Review of Education Research, 72*, 31–60.

Dougherty, K. (1987). The effects of community colleges: Aid or hindrance to socioeconomic attainment? *Sociology of Education, 60*, 86–103.

Dozier, S. B. (1993). Emotional concerns of undocumented and out-of-status foreign students. *Community Review, 13*, 33–29.

Dye, J. F., Schatz, I. M., Rosenberg, B. A., & Coleman, S. T. (2000). Constant comparison method: A kaleidoscope of data. *The Qualitative Report, 4*(1/2). Retrieved from http://www.nova.edu/ssss/QR/QR4-1/dye.html

Ferriss, S. (2010, April 1). Illegal immigrants less than 1 percent of California college enrollment. *The Sacramento Bee*, p. 1A.

Field, J. (2008). *Social capital* (2nd ed.). London, England: Routledge.

Fine, M. & Weis, L. (1996). Writing the "wrongs" of fieldwork: Confronting our own research/writing dilemmas in urban ethnographies. *Qualitative Inquiry, 2*, 251–274.

Fine, M., Weis, L., Weseen, S., & Wong, L. (2000). For whom? Qualitative research, representations, and social responsibilities. In N. K. Denzin & Y. S. Lincoln (Eds.), *Handbook of qualitative research* (2nd ed., pp. 107–131). Thousand Oaks, CA: Sage.

Flores, S. M. (2010). State dream acts: The effect of in-state resident tuition policies and undocumented Latino students. *The Review of Higher Education, 33*, 239–283.

Flores, S. M., & Chapa, J. (2009). Latino immigrant access to higher education in a bipolar context of reception. *Journal of Hispanic Higher Education, 8*, 90–109.

Flores, S. M., & Horn, C. L. (2009). College persistence among undocumented students at a selective public university: A quantitative case study analysis. *Journal of College Student Retention: Research, Theory & Practice, 11*, 57–76.

Flores, S. M., & Oseguera, L. (2009). The community college and undocumented immigrant students across state contexts: Localism and public policy. *Yearbook of the National Society for the Study of Education, 108*(1), 219–244.

Fontana, A., & Frey, J. H. (2000). The interview: From structured questions to negotiated text. In N. K. Denzin & Y. S. Lincoln (Eds.), *Handbook of qualitative research* (2nd ed., pp. 645–672). Thousand Oaks, CA: Sage Publications.

Gandara, P. (1995). *Over the ivy walls: the educational mobility of low income Chicanos.* Albany: State University of New York Press.

Garcia, L. D., & Tierney, W. G. (2011). Undocumented immigrants in higher education: A preliminary analysis. *Teachers College Record, 113*, 2739–2776.

Gildersleeve, R. E. (2010, Winter). Access between and beyond borders. *The Journal of College Admission*, 3–10.

Gladieux, L., & Swail, W. S. (1999). Financial aid is not enough: Improving the odds for minority and low-income students. In J. E. King (Ed.),

Financing a college education: How it works, how it's changing (pp. 177–197). Phoenix, AZ: American Council on Education/Oryx Press.

Glaser, B. G. & Strauss, A. L. (1967). *The discovery of grounded theory: Strategies for qualitative research.* New York, NY: Aldine Transaction.

Glesne, C., & Peshkin, P. (1992). *Becoming qualitative researchers: An introduction.* New York, NY: Longman.

Golafshani, N. (2003). Understanding reliability and validity in qualitative research. *The Qualitative Report, 8,* 597–607.

Gonzales, R. G. (2007). *Wasted talent and broken dreams: The lost potential of undocumented students.* Washington, DC: Immigration Policy Center.

Gonzales, R. G. (2009). *Young lives on hold: The college dreams of undocumented students.* New York, NY: College Board Advocacy.

Gonzalez, M. S., Plata, O., Garcia, E., Torres, M., & Urrieta, L. (2003). Testimonios de immigrantes: Students educating future teachers. *Journal of Latinos and Education, 2,* 233–243.

Granovetter, M. S. (1973). The strength of weak ties. *The American Journal of Sociology, 78*(6), 1360–1380.

Granovetter, M. S. (1982). The strength of weak ties: A network theory revisited. In P. V. Marsden & N. Lin (Eds.), *Social structure and network analysis* (pp. 105–130). Beverly Hills, CA: Sage.

Grubb, W. N. (1991). The decline of transfer rates: Evidence from national longitudinal surveys. *Journal of Higher Education 62,* 194–217.

Harrison, J., MacGibbon, L., & Morton, M. (2001). Regimes of trustworthiness in qualitative research: The rigors of reciprocity. *Qualitative Inquiry, 7,* 323–345.

Hart, D. W. (1997). *Undocumented in L.A.* Wilmington, DE: Scholarly Resources.

Heller, D. E. (1997). Student price response in higher education: An update to Leslie and Brinkman. *Journal of Higher Education, 68,* 624–659.

Heller, D. E. (1999). The effects of tuition and state financial aid on public college enrollment. *Review of Higher Education, 23,* 65–89.

Heller, J. (2009, June 11). California's 'gold standard' for higher education falls upon hard times. *The Chronicle of Higher Education.* Retrieved from http://chronicle.com/article/Californias-Gold-Standard/44468/

Hermes, J. (2008). BIG DREAMS: Serious Implications3. *Community College Journal, 78*(4), 16–17.

Hill, L., & Hayes, J. (2013, February). *Just the facts: Undocumented immigrants.* San Francisco, CA: Public Policy Institute of California.

Horvat, E. M. (2001). Understanding equity and access in higher education: The potential contribution of Pierre Bourdieu. In J. C. Smart (Ed.), *Higher education: Handbook of theory and research* (Vol. 16, pp. 195–238). New York, NY: Agathon Press.

Horvat, E. M., Weininger, E. B., & Lareau, A. (2003). Social ties to social capital: Class differences in the relations between schools and parent networks. *American Educational Research Journal, 40*, 319–351.

Hurtado, S., Carter, D. F., & Spuler, A. (1996). Latino student transition to college: Assessing difficulties and factors in successful college adjustment. *Research in Higher Education, 37*, 135–157.

Hurtado, S., Milem, J., Clayton-Pedersen, A., & Allen, W. (1999). *Enacting diverse learning environments: Improving the climate for racial/ethnic diversity in higher education.* San Francisco, CA: Jossey-Bass.

Jefferies, J. (2009). Do undocumented students play by the rules? Meritocracy in the media. *Critical Inquiry in Language Studies, 61*, 15–38.

Kane, T. J. (1999). *The price of admission: Rethinking how Americans pay for college.* Washington, DC: Brookings Institution Press.

Kao, G. (2004). Social capital and its relevance to minority and immigrant populations. *Sociology of Education, 77*, 172–183.

Keller, G. (2001). The new demographics of higher education. *The Review of Higher Education, 24*, 219–235.

Kim, D. H., & Schneider, B. (2005). Social capital in action: Alignment of parental support in adolescents' transition to postsecondary education. *Social Forces, 84*, 1181–1206.

Kvale, S. (2007). *Doing interviews.* Los Angeles, CA: Sage.

Lareau, A. (2001). Linking Bourdieu's concept of capital to the broader field: The case of family-school relationships. In B. J. Biddle (Ed.), *Social class, poverty, and education: Policy and practice* (pp. 77–100). New York, NY: Routledge.

Lareau, A., & Horvat, E. M. (1999). Moments of social inclusion and exclusion: Race, class, and cultural capital in family-school relationships. *Sociology of Education, 72*, 37–53.

Lin, N. (1999). Building a network theory of social capital. *Connections, 22*(1), 28–51

Lincoln, Y. S., & Guba, E. G. (1985). *Naturalistic inquiry*. Newbury Park, CA: Sage.

Lopez, N. (2003). *Hopeful girls, troubled boys: Race and gender disparity in urban education*. New York, NY: Routledge.

Madera, G., Mathay, A. A., Najafi, A. M., Saldivar, H. H., Solis, S., Titong, A. J. M., et al. (2008). *Underground undergrads: UCLA undocumented immigrant students speak out*. Los Angeles: University of California, Los Angeles Center for Labor Research and Education.

Marshall, T. H. (1998). Citizenship and social class. In G. Shafir (Ed.), *The citizenship debates: A reader*. Minneapolis: University of Minnesota Press.

Marx, K. (1849/1978). Wage labour and capital. In R. C. Tucker (Ed.), *The Marx-Engels reader* (2nd ed., pp. 203–217). New York, NY: W. W. Norton.

Mathison, S. (1988). Why triangulate? *Educational Researcher, 17*(2), 13–17.

Maxwell, J. A. (1996). *Qualitative research design*. Newbury Park, CA: Sage.

Melguizo, T., Hagedorn, L.S., & Cypers, S. (2008). The need for remedial/developmental education and the cost of community college transfer: Calculations from a sample of California community college transfers. *The Review of Higher Education, 31*, 401–431.

Merriam, S. (1988). *Case study research in education: A qualitative approach*. San Francisco, CA: Jossey-Bass.

Morrow, V. (1999). Conceptualising social capital in relation to the well-being of children and young people: A critical review. *The Sociological Review, 47*, 744–765.

Musoba, G., & Baez, B. (2009). The cultural capital of cultural and social capital: An economy of translations. In J. C. Smart (Ed.), *Higher education: Handbook of theory and research* (Vol. 24, pp. 151–182). Amsterdam, Netherlands: Springer.

Nash, R. (1999). Bourdieu, 'habitus', and educational research: Is it all worth the candle? *British Journal of Sociology of Education, 20*, 175–187.

National Immigration Law Center. (2009, February). *Basic facts about in-state tuition for undocumented immigrant students.* Retrieved from http://www.nilc.org/immlawpolicy/DREAM/instate-tuition-basicfacts-2009-02-23.pdf

Negron-Gonzalez, G. (2009). *Hegemony, ideology & oppositional consciousness: Undocumented youth and the personal-political struggle for educational justice* (ISSC Fellows Working Paper No. 36). Berkeley: University of California, Institute for the Study of Social Change.

Newman, I., & Benz, C. R. (1998). *Qualitative-quantitative research methodology: Exploring the interactive continuum.* Carbondale: Southern Illinois University Press.

Olivas, M. A. (2005). Plyer v. Doe, The education of undocumented children, and the polity. In D. A. Martin & P. H. Schuck (Eds.), *Immigration stories* (pp. 197–220). New York, NY: Foundation Press.

Olivas, M. A. (2009). Undocumented college students, taxation, and financial aid: A technical note. *Review of Higher Education, 32*, 407–416.

Olivas, M. A. (2012). *No undocumented child left behind: Plyler v. Doe and the education of undocumented schoolchildren.* New York, NY: NYU Press.

Oliverez, P. M. (2006). *Ready but restricted: An examination of the challenges of college access and financial aid for college-ready undocumented students in the U.S.* (Doctoral dissertation). Retrieved from ProQuest Dissertations and Theses. (UMI No. 3257819)

Onwuegbuzie, A. J., & Leech, N. L. (2007). Validity and qualitative research: An oxymoron? *Quality & Quantity, 41*, 233–249.

Orner, P. (Ed.). (2008). *Undocumented America: Narratives of undocumented lives.* San Francisco, CA: McSweeney's Books.

Passel, J. S. (2003). *Further demographic information relating to the DREAM Act.* Washington, DC: The Urban Institute.

Passel, J. S. (2005). *Unauthorized migrants: Numbers and characteristics.* Washington, DC: Pew Hispanic Center.

Passel, J. S., & Cohn, D. (2008). *Trends in unauthorized immigration: Undocumented inflow now trails legal inflow.* Washington, DC: Pew Hispanic Center.

Passel, J. S., & Cohn, D. (2009). *A portrait of unauthorized immigrants in the United States.* Washington, DC: Pew Hispanic Center.

Passel, J. S., & Cohn, D. (2011). *Unauthorized immigrant population: National and state trends, 2010.* Washington, DC: Pew Hispanic Center.

Passel, J. S., & Cohn, D. (2012, December 6). *Unauthorized immigrants: 11.1 million in 2011.* Washington, DC: Pew Hispanic Center.

Passel, J. S., Lopez, M. H. (2012, August 14). *Up to 1.7 million unauthorized immigrant youth may benefit from new deportation rules.* Washington, DC: Pew Hispanic Center.

Pastor, M., & Ortiz, R. (2009). *Immigrant integration in Los Angeles: Strategic directions for funders.* Los Angeles: Program for Environmental and Regional Equity & Center for the Study of Immigrant Integration, University of Southern California.

Perez, W. (2009). *We are Americans: Undocumented students pursuing the American Dream.* Sterling, VA: Stylus Publishing.

Perez, W. (2012). *Americans by heart: Undocumented Latino students and the promise of higher education.* New York, NY: Teachers College Press.

Perez, W., & Cortez, R. D. (2011). *Undocumented Latino college students: Their socioemotional and academic experiences.* New York, NY: LFB Scholarly.

Perez, W., Espinoza, R., Ramos, K., Coronado, H. M., & Cortes, R. (2009). Academic resilience among undocumented Latino students. *Hispanic Journal of Behavioral Sciences, 31,* 149–181.

Perez, W., Espinoza, R., Ramos, K., Coronado, H., & Cortes, R. (2010). Civic engagement patters of undocumented Mexican students. *Journal of Hispanic Higher Education, 9,* 245–265.

Perez Huber, L. (2009). Challenging racist nativist framing: Acknowledging the community cultural wealth of undocumented Chicana college students to reframe the immigration debate. *Harvard Educational Review, 79,* 704–729.

Perna, L. W. (2005). The benefits of higher education: Sex, racial/ethnic, and socioeconomic group differences. *The Review of Higher Education, 29,* 23–52.

Perry, A. M. (2006). Toward a theoretical framework for membership: The case of undocumented immigrants and financial aid for postsecondary education. *The Review of Higher Education, 30*, 21–40.

Pew Hispanic Center. (2013, January 29). *A nation of immigrants: A portrait of the 40 million, including 11 million unauthorized.* Washington, DC: Author.

Plyler v. Doe, 457 U.S. 202 (1982).

Portes, A. (1998). Social capital: Its origins and applications in modern sociology. *Annual Review of Sociology, 24*, 1–24.

Portes, A. (2000). The two meanings of social capital. *Sociological Forum, 15*, 1–12.

Portes, A., & Landolt, P. (1996, May 1). The downside of social capital. *The American Prospect, 7*(26), 18–22.

Putnam, R. D. (1995). Bowling alone: America's declining social capital. *The Journal of Democracy, 6*(1), 65–78.

Ream, R. K. (2005). Toward understanding how social capital mediates the impact of mobility on Mexican American achievement. *Social Forces, 84*, 201–224.

Reason, P. (1994). Three approaches to participative inquiry. In N. K. Denzin & Y. S. Lincoln (Eds.), *Handbook of qualitative research* (pp. 324–339). Thousand Oaks, CA: Sage.

Rincon, A. (2008). *Undocumented immigrants and higher education: Sí se puede!* New York, NY: LFB Scholarly Publishing.

Rolfe, G. (2006). Validity, trustworthiness and rigour: Quality and the idea of qualitative research. *Journal of Advanced Nursing, 53*, 304–310.

Salganik, M. J., & Heckathorn, D. D. (2004). Sampling and estimation in hidden populations using respondent-driven sampling. *Sociological Method, 34*, 193–239.

Seif, H. (2004). "Wise up!" Undocumented Latino youth, Mexican-American legislators, and the struggle for higher education access. *Latino Studies, 2*, 210–230.

Shaw, K. M. (1997). Remedial education as ideological battleground: Emerging remedial education policies in the community college. *Educational Evaluation and Policy Analysis, 19*, 284–296.

Solorzano, D., Allen, W., & Carroll, G. (2002). A case study of racial microaggressions and campus racial climate at the University of California, Berkeley. *UCLA Chicano/Latino Law Review, 23*, 15–111.

Spradley, J. P. (1979). *The ethnographic interview*. Belmont, CA: Wadsworth.

Spradley, J. P. (1980). *Participant observation*. Orlando, FL: Harcourt College Publishers.

St. John, E. P. (2003). *Refinancing the college dream: Access, equal opportunity, and justice for taxpayers*. Baltimore, MD: Johns Hopkins University Press.

St. John, E. P. (2006). Contending with financial inequality: Rethinking the contributions of qualitative research to the policy discourse on college access. *The American Behavioral Scientist, 49*, 1604–1619.

Stanton-Salazar, R. D. (1997). A social capital framework for understanding the socialization of racial minority children and youths. *Harvard Educational Review, 67*, 1–40.

Stanton-Salazar, R. D., & Dornbusch, S. M. (1995). Social capital and the reproduction of inequality: Information networks among Mexican-origin high school students. *Sociology of Education, 68*, 116–135.

Stripling, J. (2009, July 13). Tarnished jewel. *Inside Higher Ed*. Retrieved from http://www.insidehighered.com/news/2009/07/13/california1

Suarez-Orozco, C. &, Suarez-Orozco, M. M. (2001). *Children of immigration*. Cambridge, MA: Harvard University Press.

Teranishi, R., & Briscoe, K. (2006). Social capital and the racial stratification of college opportunity. In J. C. Smart (Ed.), *Higher education handbook of theory and research* (Vol. 21, pp. 591–614). Amsterdam, Netherlands: Springer.

Tierney, W. G. (2006). *Trust and the public good: Examining the cultural conditions of academic work*. New York, NY: Peter Lang.

Tierney, W. G., & Hallett, R. E. (2010). Writing on the margins from the center: Homeless youth + politics at the borders. *Cultural Studies <=> Critical Methodologies, 10*, 19–27.

Tierney, W. G., & Venegas, K. M. (2006). Fictive kin and social capital: The role of peer groups in applying and paying for college. *The American Behavioral Scientist, 49*, 1687–1702.

Tyler, S. A. (1986). Post-modern ethnography: From document of the occult to occult document. In J. Clifford & G. E. Marcus (Eds.), *Writing culture: The poetics and politics of ethnography* (pp. 122–140). Berkeley: The University of California Press.

University of California. (2007). *Major features of the California Master Plan for Higher Education.* Retrieved from http://www.ucop.edu/acadinit/mastplan/mpsummary.htm

University of California. (2010, September). *Annual report on AB 540 tuition exemptions 2008–09 academic year.* Retrieved from http://www.ucop.edu/sas/sfs/docs/ab540_annualrpt_2010.pdf

Watters, J. K., & Biernacki, P. (1989). Targeted sampling: Options for the study of hidden populations. *Social Problems, 36,* 416–430.

Weis, L., & Fine, M. (2000) *Speed bumps: A student-friendly guide to qualitative research.* New York, NY: Teachers College Press.

Zhou, M. (1997). Growing up American: The challenge confronting immigrant children and children of immigrants. *Annual Review of Sociology, 23,* 63–95.

Index